ECONOMICS OF THE FAMILY

Economics of the Family

ALESSANDRO CIGNO

CLARENDON PRESS · OXFORD

1991

Oxford University Press, Walton Street, Oxford OX2 6DP

Oxford New York Toronto
Delhi Bombay Calcutta Madras Karachi
Petaling Jaya Singapore Hong Kong Tokyo
Nairobi Dar es Salaam Cape Town
Melbourne Auckland

and associated companies in
Berlin Ibadan

Oxford is a trade mark of Oxford University Press

Published in the United States
by Oxford University Press, New York

British Library Cataloguing in Publication Data
data available

Library of Congress Cataloging in Publication Data
Cigno, Alessandro.
Economics of the family / Alessandro Cigno.
Includes bibliographical references and index.
1. Households—Economic aspects. 2. Family demography—Economic
aspects. I. Title.
HB851.C49   1991   339.2'2—dc20   91–6319
ISBN 0–19–828709–7

Set by Hope Services (Abingdon) Ltd
Printed in Great Britain by
Biddles Ltd
Guildford & King's Lynn

Contents

Contents

Introduction

> I anticipate that many sensitive, thoughtful people will be offended by these studies . . . because they may see them as debasing the family . . . These highly personal activities . . . may seem to be far beyond the realm of the economic calculus.
>
> (Schultz 1974)

Thus wrote the 1979 Nobel Prize-winner Theodore W. Schultz in his introduction to a path-breaking collection of essays on the economics of the family. Sixteen years on, many sensitive, thoughtful people continue to be offended by the application of economic reasoning to matters related to the family, while others, including some economists, regard it as, at best, a mild form of eccentricity.

The antipathy of those who have not had the benefit of an economics education for the association of the word 'economics' with the word 'family' is understandable, because economics is associated in most people's mind with money-making, commercial transactions, and self-interest in the narrowest sense. The scepticism of some economists is less easy to understand, because economics is much more than money and commerce: it is, essentially, a method for generating empirically falsifiable predictions about human behaviour under the assumption that, on average, individuals and organizations behave coherently with their own preferences (which need not be selfish), and for verifying the mutual compatibility of decisions taken by different individuals and organizations.

True, market activities and transactions between selfish individuals have traditionally been the main field of application of economics. But, increasingly, economists have been developing methods for dealing with non-market activities and with situations where preferences are altruistic in the sense that the decision-maker derives satisfaction from the happiness or well-being of others. Furthermore, market activities and the functioning of markets cannot be properly understood without a clear picture of how families and other households function. The supply of labour and the demand for consumer goods are the result of decisions taken by individuals organized in households of one kind or another. Similarly, a large part of the supply of and demand for credit comes from households. Indeed, at its most complex, the family is in competition with the capital market for the business of organizing transactions between borrowers and lenders.

Another major field of application of the economic method —public finance or, more generally, public policy—is also intimately connected with household behaviour. Since a very substantial part of public expenditure consists either of direct transfers to households—particularly to families—or of items related to the provision of services to the same, and since an equally substantial part of public revenue derives from taxes imposed on households, it is clear that the budgetary and welfare consequences of public intervention depend, in large measure, on the responses of families and other households to public policy. It goes without saying that understanding such responses is necessary for designing policy optimally.

It is not, therefore, the economic relevance of household organization and behaviour—even when looked at from the narrow point of view of the traditional interests of economists—that can be in any doubt. What may be questioned is whether individuals behave, even on average, coherently with their preferences when engaging in emotionally charged undertakings such as finding a mate, raising a child, or looking after an elderly relative. If that condition were not satisfied, families would not be susceptible to economic analysis. The statistical evidence gathered since economists began to be interested in the family does, however, suggest that, in this field also, observed behaviour tends to be consistent with the postulates of economic reasoning.

This preamble makes it easier to say what this book tries to do, and what it does not try to do. It does not presume to say anything that could be of use for predicting the behaviour of any named family or individual. It does aspire, however, to establish functional relationships that will help explain observed changes of aggregate family behaviour, and differences of behaviour between broadly defined categories of families and individuals. It also sets out to examine the congruity of various kinds of public policy aimed at the family with the declared objectives of those policies.

While trying to do justice to the main strands of thought in the burgeoning economic literature on the family—and, in particular, to the work of Gary Becker, from which much of that literature springs—the present book is not a survey of published work on the subject. It is, rather, an attempt to reproduce the main propositions of the economic theory of the family, and to generate some new ones, within a unified analytical framework—the simplest possible. Those propositions are constantly related to the evidence, but the references to the empirical literature are intended to be illustrative rather than anywhere near exhaustive. For reasons of familiarity, rather than vanity, the author's own contributions loom disproportionately large.

Finally, a word about the style of presentation. In writing about families, one is tempted to try to appeal not only to students and practitioners of one's own discipline, but also to all who have an intellectual or professional interest in the subject. That, however, is always fraught with danger, because one risks boring the former with explanations of elementary concepts, while still baffling the latter. The present book is thus aimed at readers acquainted with the methods of modern microeconomics, particularly at senior students of economics. That notwithstanding, plain English is substituted for economic jargon wherever possible, and analytical results are explained in intuitive terms, in the hope that even the reader who cannot follow the technical arguments can at least get a feeling for what economics has to say about this important subject.

PART I

Household Formation and Marriage

1

Matchmaking

Of the two main events in the life of a family—marriage and reproduction—the former is the one which would have appeared more susceptible to economic analysis in days gone by, when marriage was generally regarded as too serious a business to be left to the proclivities and clouded judgement of the interested parties. Those were, and in some traditional societies still are, the days when parents took a major part in finding marriage partners for their children, and dowry-bargaining was common practice. By contrast, now that young people tend to gain independence from their parents at an earlier age, it might be argued that the rationality assumptions underlying the economic approach are totally inappropriate to explaining why two persons decide to marry.

It is doubtful, however, whether the decision by a particular individual to buy a particular brand of a particular product at a particular time is any more rational (i.e. consistent with that person's preferences, given the constraints) than the decision to marry a particular person at a particular date. Indeed, it could be argued that today's freer relations between the sexes and the greater ease with which legal marriages can be dissolved in most countries make it more, rather than less, realistic to regard the married state as the result of a free, informed, and optimizing choice—in other words, that two persons marry and stay married because, on balance, they are better off that way.

In the present chapter, we examine a particularly simple explanation of how people are matched with members of the opposite sex. The picture will become progressively richer and more complicated in subsequent chapters.

1.1. *A Simple Marriage Game*

Suppose there are N men and N women, each of whom has a preference ranking for all members of the opposite sex. How will they be matched (under the assumption of monogamy)? As is customary in economics, we shall try to answer this question by looking for an *equilibrium*, i.e. in the present context, for a situation where no individual is willing and able to change marriage partner. Analytically, the problem is no different from that of matching trading partners, or employers with employees.

Since an individual gains utility by co-operating with another (of the opposite sex), we can think of the match-making problem as a simple form of *co-operative game*.[1] A suitable equilibrium concept for this type of game is the *core*, defined in the present context as the set of all feasible allocations which cannot be blocked (improved upon) by any player or pair of players. Assuming, for the moment, that each player prefers to marry the least attractive member of the opposite sex rather than remaining single, a feasible allocation is simply a sorting of the players into couples: a description of which male is paired off with which female. An allocation can be blocked if a man and a woman are happier marrying each other rather than the allotted partners.

For example, suppose that there are three men, labelled m_1, m_2, and m_3, and three women, labelled f_1, f_2, and f_3. Suppose, further, that their preferences are represented by the matrix

$$\mathbf{R} = \begin{array}{c} \\ m_1 \\ m_2 \\ m_3 \end{array} \begin{array}{ccc} f_1 & f_2 & f_3 \\ \begin{bmatrix} 1,1 & 2,1 & 3,1 \\ 1,2 & 2,2 & 3,2 \\ 1,3 & 2,3 & 3,3 \end{bmatrix} \end{array}$$

The first digit in cell (m,f), where $m = m_1, m_2, m_3$ and $f = f_1, f_2, f_3$, indicates the position of woman f in the preference ranking of man m, while the second digit indicates the position of man m in the preference ranking of woman f.

Thus, in this example, m_1 prefers f_1 to f_2 and f_2 to f_3, while f_1 prefers m_1 to m_2 and m_2 to m_3, etc. The feasible allocations are

$$A_1 = \{m_1f_1, \ m_2f_2, \ m_3f_3\}$$
$$A_2 = \{m_1f_2, \ m_2f_1, \ m_3f_3\}$$
$$A_3 = \{m_1f_3, \ m_2f_2, \ m_3f_1\}$$
$$A_4 = \{m_1f_3, \ m_3f_2, \ m_2f_1\}$$
$$A_5 = \{m_1f_1, \ m_3f_2, \ m_2f_3\}$$
$$A_6 = \{m_1f_2, \ m_2f_3, \ m_3f_1\}$$

Given **R**, we can construct for each allocation a diagraph (Fig. 1.1), indicating by an arrow from one individual to another of the opposite sex a preference of the first for the second over the partner assigned by the present allocation. Thus, in A_1, m_2 is matched with f_2 but would prefer to marry f_1, while f_2 would prefer to marry m_1, etc. In A_2, m_1 is matched with f_2 but prefers f_1, who in turn prefers m_1 to her partner m_2. The presence of this loop indicates that A_2 is not in the core, because it would be blocked by m_1 marrying f_1. Since A_3, A_4, A_5, and A_6 can also be blocked by one or more couples breaking ranks and marrying each other instead of their assigned partners, it is clear that the only core allocation is A_1.

A_1 is an equilibrium because, although some of the men and women would prefer a different partner, the object of their desire would not agree to the match. It can be shown that the core of the marriage game is always non-empty and, therefore, that at least one equilibrium allocation exists.[2] In general, however, the core may contain more than one allocation[3]—as the next example will show.

1.2. *Assortative Mating?*

Do people tend to marry their equals (assortative mating) in the sense that they tend to end up with marriage partners of similar attractiveness?[4] That would certainly be the case if

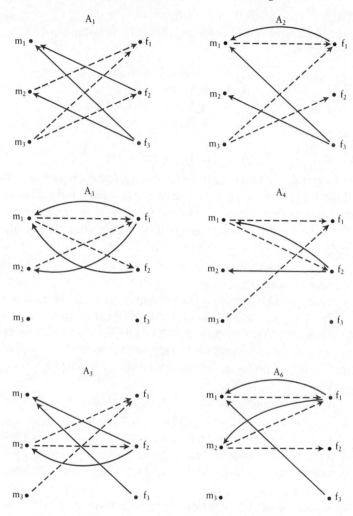

FIG. 1.1

a person's ranking of members of the opposite sex were based on only one consideration, such as wealth, and everyone agreed that more is better than less. In the example given in the last section, if we suppose that m_1 is richer than m_2, and m_2 than m_3—and similarly that f_1 is richer than f_2, and f_2 than f_3—it is clear that the richest boy marries the richest girl, the second richest boy marries the second richest girl, and so on.

What if a person's attractiveness depends on several of his or her characteristics (wealth, looks, personality, etc.)? If all members of the same sex had the same tastes, they would still be unanimous in their rankings. In that case the outcome would still be that the most desirable boy marries the most desirable girl, and so on down the line, but 'most desirable' would not necessarily mean richest.

If tastes differ, assortative mating must be defined more tightly because there is no unanimity about rankings. A suitable definition would be 'each husband occupies the same position in his wife's ranking of males, that she occupies in his ranking of females'.

Suppose, for example, that

$$\mathbf{R} = \begin{array}{c} \\ m_1 \\ m_2 \\ m_3 \end{array} \begin{array}{ccc} f_1 & f_2 & f_3 \\ \begin{bmatrix} 1,1 & 2,1 & 3,1 \\ 3,3 & 1,3 & 2,2 \\ 3,2 & 2,2 & 1,3 \end{bmatrix} \end{array}$$

This example differs from the previous one in that people differ in the way they rank their potential mates. The possible allocations are the same as in the first example, but the diagraphs have changed (see Fig. 1.2). A_5 is now an 'assorted' allocation (m_1 and f_1 are each other's first choice, while m_3 and f_2 and m_2 and f_1 are each other's second choice) and a solution of the game, but it is not unique: the core contains one other allocation, A_1, which is not assorted. The outcome is thus just as likely to be non-assorted as assorted.

Does it matter whether marriages are assorted or not? It certainly does if marriage candidates agree in their ranking of potential partners, for in that case the better endowed will make the better catches, and happiness will become more unequally distributed as a result of marriage. In particular, if preference rankings were based on wealth

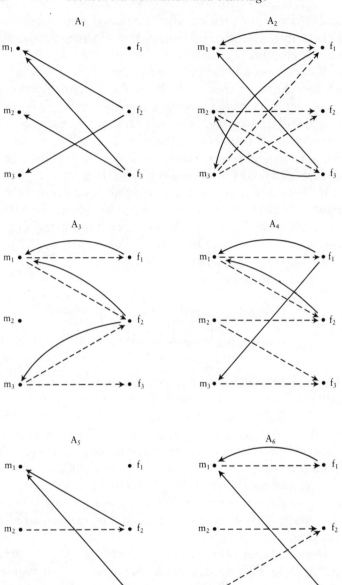

F ig. 1.2

alone, and everyone agreed that more is better than less, then marriage would reinforce economic inequality. If, on the other hand, rankings are based on more than one characteristic or people differ in their preferences, then there is no reason to expect that marriage will necessarily reinforce wealth inequality, or make happiness less equally distributed.

1.3. *Courting*

Granted that there is at least a solution to the marriage game, how will it be realized? One possibility is to have a professional matchmaker (the equivalent of the auctioneer in Walrasian markets) who makes enquiries about peoples' preferences and works out a solution. Another is to leave the interested parties to search for themselves: provided that search is costless, and provided that nobody commits himself or herself to marrying before all the alternatives are tested or, equivalently, that promises of marriage can be broken without any cost or disutility, then a core solution may eventually be reached.

A ritualized search or 'courting' procedure might be as follows: (i) let each man propose to his favourite woman; (ii) let each proposed-to woman keep her best suitor waiting and reject all others; (iii) let each rejected man propose to his next favourite woman; (iv) repeat steps (ii) and (iii) until either there are no rejected men left, or every rejected man has exhausted the list of women. An alternative to this male chauvinist procedure would be a liberated one, with the word 'woman' substituted for 'man' throughout.[5] Either will seek out a core allocation. Indeed, one of the ways in which the existence of at least one solution to the marriage game can be demonstrated is by showing that such procedures yield an unblockable allocation.[6]

In the following chapters we shall enrich this simple model of 'marriage' by looking more closely at the benefits and costs that an individual may derive from entering into this particular form of partnership with another individual, at the costs and benefits of continuing or curtailing the search, and at those of resuming it.

NOTES

1. For a classical exposition of the mathematical theory of games, with many interesting applications, see Luce and Raiffa (1957). The present application to the marriage problem is owed to Dolton (1982).
2. See Dolton (1982) for proof and various extensions.
3. See Dolton (1982) for uniqueness conditions.
4. In the economics literature on marriage the expressions 'assortative mating' or 'positive assortative mating' are more often used, somewhat confusingly, to indicate positive correlation between the levels at which a particular characteristic (e.g. wealth, earning ability, or education) is present in both spouses; see, particularly, Becker (1973, 1974, 1981). As is made clear below and again in Chap. 4, assortative mating in one sense does not necessarily imply assortative mating in the other.
5. Interested readers are invited to check for themselves that, where more than one core allocation exists, as in the example of the last section, the male-chauvinist and the liberated courting routines lead to different solutions.
6. This was done, for the male-chauvinist routine, by Gale and Shapley (1962). The proof of convergence for the liberated routine is perfectly analogous. Dolton's proof of the existence of at least one equilibrium solution is more general, as it does not rely on any particular courting routine: he simply demonstrates that the marriage game is 'balanced' in the sense of formal game theory (according to which, the core of any balanced game is non-empty).

2

Home-Production

In the last chapter, we saw how a group of men and women bent on marriage would sort themselves into couples on the basis of their preference rankings. With a little ingenuity, that type of analysis can be extended to the case where one sex is numerically stronger than the other—in which case some of the participants in the marriage game must necessarily remain single—or to that where some might actually choose to remain single even if a willing partner could be found. But, if we want to go further and find out how the sorting is affected by personal characteristics and the economic environment, we must first take a step back and investigate how personal characteristics and the economic environment affect the costs and benefits of marriage. Furthermore, we must be able to compare the costs and benefits of marriage with those of singleness.

In pursuing this line of enquiry, we shall find it fruitful to view the household as an organization producing goods of various kinds for the benefit of its own members, and to compare the efficiency of this productive process in households of different type and size. Such an approach draws its origins from Gary Becker's insight[1] that market commodities are not consumed in their raw state, but transformed into utility-giving final goods[2] (not transferable from one household to another) by the application of the consumer's own time. For example, a meal at home requires various ingredients and appliances to prepare it, and time in which to prepare and consume it. We may, therefore, think of the good 'home meal' as having been produced by household members using as inputs market commodities and their own time. Such a product will have different characteristics and generally yield different utility from a restaurant meal. Typically, it will also have different monetary and time costs. Its costs and characteristics will vary also according to the number of people involved and to the relationship that exists among them: cooking for two is generally more efficient than cooking for one, and eating alone or in the company of strangers is not the same as sitting down to a family dinner!

The home-production approach thus outlined has considerable generality and includes as a special case the standard consumer model of microeconomic theory, where commodities bought from the market are assumed to be consumed without any further processing and without any expenditure of the consumer's own time. Another special case is the income-leisure model, widely used in labour economics and macroeconomics, according to which the good 'leisure' is domestically produced by time alone, without any input of commodities. By allowing negative inputs (i.e. outputs) of commodities, the home-production approach can be extended to households producing commodities for the market along with goods for own consumption.

2.1. *One-Person Households*

Let us start by considering a household consisting of just one person, j. The production possibilities open to this household are summarized by a *home-production function* $F(\ )$, such that

$$X_j = F(H_j, I_j), \tag{2.1}$$

where X_j is an aggregate measure of domestic output, Hj the amount of j's time dedicated to domestic production activities, and I_j an aggregate measure of the quantities of commodities bought from the market.

It seems reasonable to assume that the home-production function is quasi-concave, and that its isoquants do not cut the axes—in other words that both time and commodities are essential to the domestic production of goods, but that they are substitutable for each other at a diminishing marginal rate. Since there are no other factors of production besides time and commodities, it is also natural to suppose that the home-production function is linear-homogeneous, i.e. that an equiproportionate increase in the inputs of these two factors would cause output to rise by the same proportion.[3] In the present context, this is tantamount to saying that home-production is characterized by constant returns to scale, but we shall see later that it leaves scope for economies or diseconomies of scale if scale is expressed in number of household members.

The choice of H_j and I_j is subject to a number of restrictions. First, neither variable can be negative. Second, home-time must satisfy

$$H_j \leqslant T, \tag{2.2}$$

where T is the total amount of time available to each person. Third, expenditure must not exceed income,

$$I_j \leqslant w_j L_j + V_j, \tag{2.3}$$

where L_j, w_j, and V_j are, respectively, j's labour supply, wage rate, and property income, all expressed in terms of commodities. And finally, since leisure is subsumed in X_j, labour and home-time must add up to T, so that

$$L_j \equiv T - H_j. \tag{2.4}$$

In general, j will be interested in both the size and the composition of the home-product, but for our immediate purposes it may be assumed that only size matters (the choice of output mix will be examined in Part II). Since j's utility or satisfaction will rise with X_j, H_j and I_j will then be chosen so as to maximize (2.1), subject to (2.2) and to a *budget constraint*,

$$w_j H_j + I_j \leqslant w_j T + V_j \equiv Y_j \tag{2.5}$$

obtained by substituting (2.4) into (2.3) and rearranging terms. Y_j is j's *full income*.

How will time be allocated? The rate of return to L_j is given by the market wage rate w_j. The rate of return to H_j, which we shall call the *shadow-wage rate*, is none other than the marginal rate of technical substitution of commodities for home-time,

$$w_j^* \equiv \frac{F_H}{F_I}, \tag{2.6}$$

where F_H is the marginal product of home-time, and F_I the marginal product of commodities. If the shadow-wage rate exceeds the wage rate for all H_j less than T, then j's time will be used exclusively for home-production, and I_j will be equal to V_j. Otherwise, j will engage in home-production up to the point where w_j^* is equal to w_j, and use the rest of the time to raise income. Therefore, in general,

$$(w_j^* - w_j)(T - H_j) = 0. \tag{2.7}$$

The two possible outcomes are illustrated in Fig. 2.1, where the budget constraint is shown as a straight line (truncated at T) and the home-production function is represented by its highest achievable isoquant. In panel (*a*), the slope of the isoquant at T, w_j^*, is higher than the slope of the budget line, w_j, so L_j is equal to zero. In panel (*b*), by contrast, L_j is positive because the two slopes are equalized before H_j has reached T.

Now suppose that unearned income increases to V_j'. If j's time is already fully committed to home-production ($H_j = T$), the additional income will be spent entirely to buy

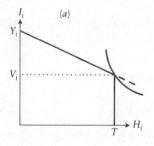 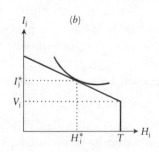

Fig. 2.1

more commodities, as shown in Fig. 2.2(*a*). Otherwise, home-time H_j will rise as shown in Fig. 2.2(*b*) (and the labour supply L_j will fall by the same amount). I_j will rise too, but by less than $(V'_j - V_j)$, because the unearned income rise is partly offset by a fall in earnings. For small changes in V_j, we may write

$$\frac{V_j}{I_j} \frac{\partial I_j}{\partial V_j} = \frac{V_j}{Y_j} \epsilon_{yi}, \qquad \epsilon_{yi} > 0 \qquad (2.8)$$

and

$$\frac{V_j}{H_j} \frac{\partial H_j}{\partial V_j} = \frac{V_j}{Y_j} \epsilon_{yj}, \qquad \epsilon_{yj} \gtrless 0, \qquad (2.9)$$

where ϵ_{yi} and ϵ_{yj} denote full-income elasticities of, respectively, commodities and home-time.

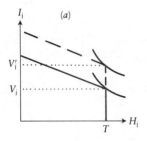 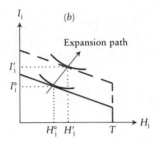

FIG. 2.2

Suppose, next, that the wage rate increases. If (2.2) is binding, then nothing else will happen. Otherwise, I_j will rise because the cross-substitution effect and the income effect are both positive, while H_j may fall (as in Fig. 2.3) or rise, depending on whether the negative substitution effect dominates or is dominated by the positive income effect. But, whether it falls or rises in absolute terms, H_j will always fall relative to I_j: X_j will be produced less time-intensively. For small wage changes, we can write, using the Slutsky decomposition of price effects,

$$\frac{w_j}{I_j}\frac{\partial I_j}{\partial w_j} = \epsilon_{hi} + \frac{w_j L_j}{Y_j}\epsilon_{yi}, \qquad \epsilon_{hi} \geqslant 0 \qquad (2.10)$$

and

$$\frac{w_j}{H_j}\frac{\partial H_j}{\partial w_j} = \epsilon_{hh} + \frac{w_j L_j}{Y_j}\epsilon_{yj}, \qquad \epsilon_{hh} \leqslant 0, \qquad (2.11)$$

where ϵ_{hi} and ϵ_{hh} denote compensated wage elasticities of, respectively, commodities and home-time.

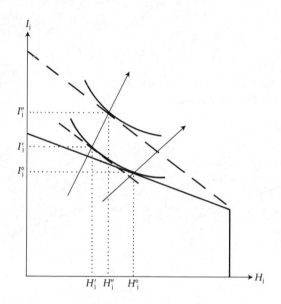

FIG. 2.3

Thus, in conclusion, if we compare two single persons only differing from each other in respect of their property income, we can expect the wealthier of the two to spend more time on home-production activities, and less in the labour market, than the other one. By contrast, if they differ only in respect of their earning ability, then the more able one will spend relatively less time on home-production than in the labour market, and produce goods at home with a relatively larger input of commodities, than the other.

2.2. Two-Person Households

We now come to the question of whether multi-person households are more efficient producers of goods than one-person households. That, notice, is not the same as asking whether each member of a multi-person household is better off than he or she would be in a separate one-person household—the answer to which depends also on how the joint product is shared out. But, a positive answer to the first of these questions is necessary for the answer to the second to be positive too.

Let us then consider two individuals, m and f (not necessarily one male and the other female), living in separate one-person households. A merger of their two households would obviously be efficient if there were opportunities for sharing common expenses, or if the two-person household resulting from the merger had access to production possibilities (e.g. making children) unavailable to the original units. First, however, we want to show that the merger may be efficient even in the absence of those obvious advantages.

Suppose, for example, that m's one-person output, maximized subject to m's one-person budget constraint, is equal to f's, similarly maximized, one-person output. Suppose, further, that V_m is less than V_f, and w_m more than w_f, so that m's efficient one-person input mix is less time-intensive than f's. In Fig. 2.4(a), m's output is maximized at the point P, with coordinates (H_m^*, I_m^*), and f's at the point Q, with coordinates (H_f^*, I_f^*). Now, consider the midpoint, R, of the line segment joining P to Q. Since R lies on a higher isoquant, output at that point is higher than at either P or Q. R is unattainable by either m or f acting independently, because it lies above their respective one-person budget constraints (represented by broken lines). It can be reached, however, by the two acting in concert: all they need to do is exchange $\frac{1}{2}(I_m^* - I_f^*)$ of m's income for $\frac{1}{2}(H_f^* - H_m^*)$ of f's time. If there were many households with these characteristics, that would give rise to a market for domestic labour.

By collaboration, m and f could thus increase their combined (and, as it happens, individual) output, while still remaining in separate one-person households. They could do even better, however, by outright merger. To see that, consider a composite household endowed with $\frac{1}{2} (V_m + V_f)$ units of property income, $\frac{1}{2} T$ units of time attracting the higher wage rate w_m, and $\frac{1}{2} T$ units of time attracting the lower wage rate w_f. The maximized output of such a household will be half that of the two-person household that would result from the merger. As shown in Fig. 2.3(*a*), the composite household will locate itself at point S of its budget boundary (represented by a continuous line) where output is higher than at R. By merging, m and f would thus have more goods to share between them than they would have, even with collaboration, if they stayed apart.

For another example, suppose that m and f have the same wage rate. If they have also the same unearned income, it is obvious that they have nothing to gain from either co-operation or merger. The same would be true—so long as the time constraint were not binding on either of them—if m and f had different property incomes, but still the same wage rate. As shown by Fig. 2.4(*b*), if V_f is higher than V_m, and the individual time constraint is at T, then m's one-person output is maximized at P, and f's at Q. Since the input mix is the same at both those points, there is clearly no scope for improving the mix by either swapping inputs or pooling resources. Not so, however, if the individual time constraint is at T', and thus binding on f's one-person household. The latter, in this case, maximizes its output at Q', where the input mix is less time intensive than at P. By co-operation, m and f could both move to R', but that would not do them any good, because output at that point is just the arithmetic mean of output at P and Q'. On the other hand, by merging, m and f could jointly produce twice the output associated with point R, and thus more than twice

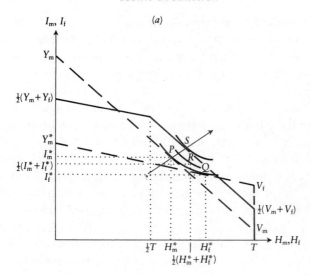

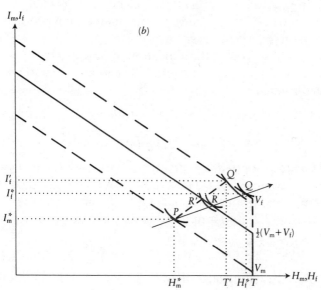

FIG. 2.4

that associated with point R'. It is then clear that merger may enhance productivity even in a case where the potential partners differ in their property endowments only.

Notice that, in each of the cases considered, the merged household produces at least as much as the two component households put together. Where it produces more, it is because the parties can pursue their comparative advantages more fully than they could without the merger. That does not mean, however, that greater efficiency is always associated with greater division of labour between the parties. It was so in the example with w_m greater than w_f, because in that case it was efficient for f to replace m, as far as possible, in home-based activities. It was not so in the one with V_f greater than V_m (and the time constraint at T'), because the whole point of merger, there, was to allow f to do exactly the same as m![4] In general, however, the efficiency gain is likely to be greater where the parties to the merger have different comparative advantages.

Let us now look at the allocation of time in a two-person household in more general terms. The joint output of goods is determined by

$$X_{mf} = F(H_{mf}, I_{mf}), \qquad (2.12)$$

where

$$H_{mf} = H_m + H_f \qquad (2.13)$$

denotes the joint input of home-time, and I_{mf} the joint input of commodities. The two household members have a common interest in maximizing (2.12), subject to the time constraint (2.2) for j = m,f, and to the *joint budget constraint*

$$w_m H_m + w_f H_f + I_{mf} \leqslant$$
$$V_m + V_f + (w_m + w_f)T \equiv Y_m + Y_f. \qquad (2.14)$$

A solution will again satisfy (2.7), for j = m,f. As in one-person households, an individual will thus participate in both market and home activities if and only if that individual's wage and shadow-wage rates are equal. In a two-person household, however, it is possible that one member will have a wage rate higher than the shadow-wage rate (common to both members of the household) and that it is thus efficient for such a person to specialize completely in paid work, leaving all the domestic chores to the other. That would obviously be impossible in a one-person household.

Fig. 2.5 illustrates the possible outcomes for the case where the household members have different wage rates. We shall continue to assume that w_m is the larger of the two, but only the subscripts would need to change if the opposite were true. In panel (a), the efficient level of the joint home-time is H_{mf}^*, less than T, and

$$w_f = w_f^* = w_m^* < w_m. \qquad (2.15)$$

Since the cheaper time will be used first in the home, this means that m specializes completely in paid work ($L_m = T$),

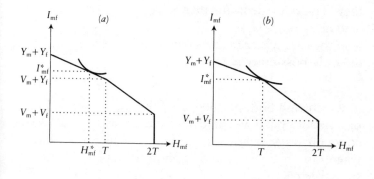

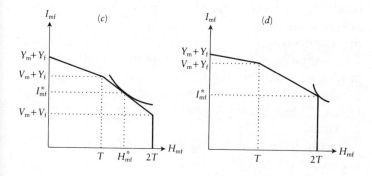

FIG. 2.5

while f spends some time at home ($H_f = H_{mf}^*$) and some in the market ($L_f = T - H_{mf}^*$). In panel (b), H_{mf}^* equals T, and

$$w_f < w_f^* = w_m^* < w_m. \qquad (2.16)$$

Here, both members are fully specialized: f at home ($H_f = T$) and m in the market ($L_m = T$). In panel (c), H_{mf}^* is more than T but less than $2T$, and

$$w_f < w_f^* = w_m^* = w_m. \qquad (2.17)$$

Hence, f is fully specialized in home work ($H_f = H_{mf} - T$), while m spends some time at home ($H_m = H_{mf}^* - T$) and some in paid work ($L_m = 2T - H_{mf}^*$). In panel (d), finally, H_{mf}^* is equal to $2T$, and

$$w_f < w_m < w_f^* = w_m^*. \qquad (2.18)$$

There, m and f have so much property between them, that they can both dedicate themselves exclusively to home activities ($H_m = H_f = T$).

In the case where m and f command the same wage rate, the only possibility is

$$w_f = w_m < w_m^* = w_m^* \qquad (2.19)$$

in which case both partners are fully specialized in home-production. What we could not have is a situation where the common wage rate is greater than the common shadow-wage rate, because both household members would then specialize completely in paid work, and no goods would be produced. Nor would there be any point in setting up a two-person household if the common wage rate were equal to the common shadow-wage rate, because both partners would then be sharing equally in both activities, and thus producing jointly no more than the sum of what they could produce separately. In conclusion, at least one household member must always specialize fully in one of the two activities.

Finally, let us consider the effects of a change in property income or in one of the wage rates. A rise in either V_m or V_f, no matter which, will lift the budget constraint, increasing I_{mf} and, unless both partners are fully specialized in home-

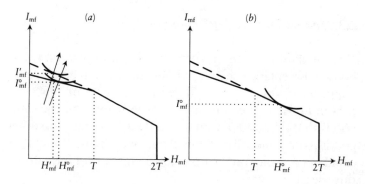

FIG. 2.6

production, H_{mf}. A rise in the lower of the two wage rates, w_f, will rotate the first segment of the budget line clockwise (see Fig. 2.6). Therefore, H_{mf} and I_{mf} will be affected if f participates in both home and market activities, but not otherwise. A rise in w_m, on the other hand, will rotate the whole budget line (see Fig. 2.7). Therefore, both H_{mf} and I_{mf} may be affected as long as at least one member of the household does some paid work. While a rise in property income is likely to reduce the household's total labour supply ($L_m + L_f$), it is thus clear that a wage rise may or may not increase it, and that the effect may be different according to which of the two wage rates has changed.

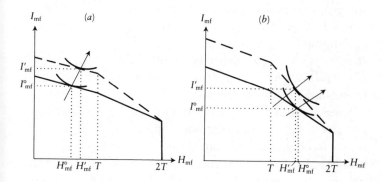

FIG. 2.7

2.3. *Sexual Division of Labour*

Now imagine a situation where the merger of two individual households enlarges the set of home-production possibilities. Suppose, in other words, that the members of this two-person household can produce not only more of the same goods that they could produce on their own, but also other goods (companionship, familiarity, love, children) that they could not produce on their own. A simple way of formalizing this idea is to write

$$H_{mf} = G^{mf}(H_m, H_f) > H_m + H_f, \qquad (2.20)$$

where $G^{mf}(\ )$ may be interpreted as another kind of home-production function.[5] It is thus as if m and f produced first an intermediate good H_{mf} by time alone in accordance with (2.20), and then combined that with commodities to produce final goods in accordance with (2.12).

If (2.20) is true—that is, the relationship between m and f is such that H_{mf} is indeed greater than the sum of H_m and H_f—it is then clear that m and f have more to gain from their association than just allocative efficiency. In the rest of this chapter we shall concentrate our attention on a special type of two-person household, the nuclear family, consisting initially of a man, m, and a woman, f (here sex matters). Such a household type lies at the opposite end of the spectrum from the purely business-like arrangement examined in the last section, where the only advantage of communal living was to replace the individual budget constraints with a less restricting joint judget. But, much of what follows applies also to the in-between cases (close friendships, loose marriages).

Suppose that $G^{mf}(\ )$ has the same general properties as $F(\ )$, including the one that both inputs, while substitutable for each other at a diminishing rate, are essential to production. That immediately rules out the possibility of either partner choosing to specialize completely in market work (or how would they keep each other company, let alone have children). Unlike $F(\ )$, however, $G^{mf}(\ )$ is specific to that particular m and f: a different pair, with different personal characteristics, might relate differently, or not at all (in which case the joint home-time would be just the sum of the parts).

Given (2.12) and (2.20), m and f will again have a common interest in making their output of final goods as large as possible, subject to a time constraint (2.2) for each of them, and to the common budget constraint (2.14). As in the situation examined in the last section, an output-maximizing allocation of time will again satisfy (2.7) for $j = m,f$. But, since the shadow-wage rates are now given by

$$w_j^* \equiv \frac{F_H}{F_I} G_j^{mf}, \qquad (2.21)$$

where G_j^{mf} is the marginal product of H_j in terms of H_{mf}, there is no reason, in general, why w_m^* should be equal to w_f^*. Consequently, it does not necessarily follow that at least one of the partners must specialize completely in one activity.

The organization of home-production can be better understood if we break the optimization process into two stages. We start by looking for the time-mix that minimizes the income forgone $(w_m H_m + w_f H_m)$ in order to attain a desired level of intermediate production H_{mf}, subject to (2.20), and to (2.2) for $j = m,f$. A solution to this cost-minimizing exercise will either equate the marginal rate of technical substitution of H_m for H_f to the wage ratio,

$$\frac{G_m^{mf}}{G_f^{mf}} = \frac{w_m}{w_f}, \qquad (2.22)$$

or set the home-time of at least one of the partners equal to T. The possibilities are illustrated in Fig. 2.8, where the curve is the isoquant of $G^{mf}(\ )$ corresponding to the desired output of the intermediate good, H_{mf}.

In panel (*a*), the isoquant is symmetric around the 45° line, implying that m and f are interchangeable in their domestic roles. In that case, the partners will share domestic

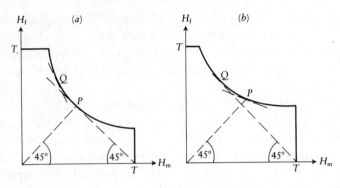

Fig. 2.8

activities equally between them (point P) if their wage rates
are the same, unequally (e.g. at point Q) if not. But, there is
no reason to expect that male and female domestic roles are
indeed interchangeable—think, for example, of the woman's
role in childbearing. In panel (b), by contrast, it is assumed
that her home-time can be more readily substituted for his,
than his for hers. Consequently, it would be efficient for her
to spend more time at home than him (e.g. to locate at point
Q) even if her wage rate were equal to his, and for both to
contribute equal shares (as at point P) only if w_f is sufficiently
higher than w_m.

Now let $W^{mf}(H_{mf}, w_m, w_f)$ denote the minimized cost of
H_{mf}, at the given values of w_m and w_f. Its partial derivative
with respect to w_j, W_j^{mf}, is the demand for H_j conditional on
the stated value of H_{mf}. The partial derivative with respect
to H_{mf}, $w_{mf} \equiv W_H^{mf}$, is the marginal cost (in lost income) of
H_{mf}. We can thus think of w_{mf} as the 'price' charged by
the household department producing the intermediate good
to the household department producing the final good. The
function $W^{mf}(\ )$ is obviously increasing in all its arguments.
Since an increase in the net wage rate of either partner
would induce a substitution of that person's home-time
with that of the other, $W^{mf}(\ )$ is concave in w_j. It is, on the
other hand, linear in H_{mf} up to a point, and then convex, as
the following reasoning demonstrates.

Given constant returns, w_{mf} is independent of H_{mf} up to the point where H_f is fully used for home-production. This is shown in Fig. 2.9, where H_m and H_f are combined in the same proportion, satisfying (2.22), and the income forgone thus rises in proportion to H_{mf} up to $\bar{H}_{fm} \equiv G^{mf}(\bar{H}_m, T)$. Further increases in the intermediate output are possible only by raising the ratio of H_m to H_f, and thus pushing their marginal rate of technical substitution below their wage ratio. The marginal cost will then rise until, at $\bar{\bar{H}}_{mf} \equiv G^{mf}(T, T)$, H_{mf} can grow no more, and w_{mf} goes to infinity.

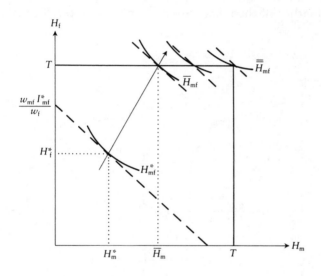

FIG. 2.9

Next, we look for the combination of commodities and joint home-time that makes the output of final goods as large as possible. The second stage of the optimization process is thus to maximize (2.12), subject to the budget constraint, which can now be written as

$$W^{mf}(H_{mf}, w_m, w_f) + I_{mf} \leqslant Y_m + Y_f. \qquad (2.14')$$

At a maximum output point, the marginal rate of technical

substitution of H_{mf} for I_{mf} is equal to the marginal cost of the intermediate product,

$$\frac{F_H}{F_I} = w_{mf}. \tag{2.23}$$

That is illustrated in Fig. 2.10, where the concave-to-the-origin curve, with absolute slope w_{mf}, represents the budget constraint, and the convex-to-the-origin curve is an isoquant of $F(\ )$. Efficiency may require both partners to share in both market and home activities as in panel (*a*), or f to dedicate herself completely to the latter as in panels (*b*) and (*c*), or both to do so as in panel (*d*), but in no circumstances will either of them specialize completely in the former.

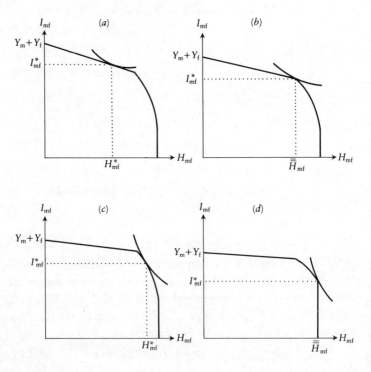

F IG . 2.10

2.4. *Effects of Income and Wage Changes in Nuclear Families*

In a nuclear family, as in any kind of household, a rise in property income lifts the budget line. I_{mf} thus increases, as does H_j if $j = m,f$ is not already fully committed to homely pursuits. For small changes

$$\frac{V_j}{I_{mf}}\frac{\partial I_{mf}}{\partial V_j} = \frac{V_j}{Y_m + Y_f}\epsilon_{yi}, \tag{2.24}$$

$$\frac{V_j}{H_m}\frac{\partial H_m}{\partial V_j} = \frac{V_j}{Y_m + Y_f}\frac{\gamma_m}{\xi_m}\epsilon_{yh}, \tag{2.25}$$

and

$$\frac{V_j}{H_f}\frac{\partial H_f}{\partial V_j} = \frac{V_j}{Y_m + Y_f}\frac{\gamma_f}{\xi_f}\epsilon_{yh}, \tag{2.26}$$

where $\epsilon_{yh} \geq 0$ and $\epsilon_{yi} > 0$ are the full-income elasticities of H_{mf} and I_{mf}, respectively, $\gamma_j > 0$ is the elasticity of w_{mf} to w_j, and

$$\xi_j \equiv \frac{w_j H_j}{w_{mf} H_{mf}}. \tag{2.27}$$

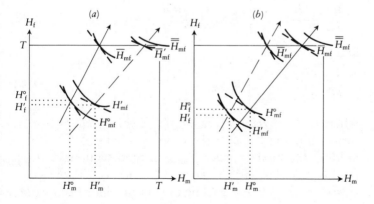

Fig. 2.11

A rise in w_f makes H_f more expensive relative to H_m, causing the expansion path of H_{mf} to rotate clockwise as in panel (*a*) of Fig. 2.11. Conversely, a rise in w_m makes H_f relatively cheaper, causing the expansion path to rotate the other way as in panel (*b*). A rise in either wage rate increases full income, but also makes H_{mf} more expensive relative to I_{mf}. Therefore, the budget line becomes everywhere steeper, as shown in Fig. 2.12. It is then clear that any wage rise will increase the demand for commodities, in absolute and relative to total home-time, but that the latter and each partner's contribution to it may fall or rise depending on the relative strengths of the full-income effect and of the two substitution effects. For small wage changes,

$$\frac{w_m}{I_{mf}} \frac{\partial I_{mf}}{\partial w_m} = \gamma_m \, \epsilon_{hi} + \frac{w_m L_f}{Y_m + Y_f} \, \epsilon_{yi}, \qquad (2.28)$$

$$\frac{w_m}{H_m} \frac{\partial H_m}{\partial w_m} = \frac{\gamma_m}{\xi_f} \left[\gamma_m \, \epsilon_{hh} + \frac{w_m L_m}{Y_m + Y_f} \, \epsilon_{yh} \right] + \eta_{mm}, \qquad (2.29)$$

$$\frac{w_m}{H_f} \frac{\partial H_f}{\partial w_m} = \frac{\gamma_f}{\xi_f} \left[\gamma_m \, \epsilon_{hh} + \frac{w_m L_m}{Y_m + Y_f} \, \epsilon_{yh} \right] + \eta_{mf}, \qquad (2.30)$$

$$\frac{w_f}{I_{mf}} \frac{\partial I_{mf}}{\partial w_f} = \gamma_f \, \epsilon_{hi} + \frac{w_f L_f}{Y_m + Y_f} \, \epsilon_{yi}, \qquad (2.31)$$

$$\frac{w_f}{H_f} \frac{\partial H_f}{\partial w_f} = \frac{\gamma_f}{\xi_f} \left[\gamma_f \, \epsilon_{hh} + \frac{w_f L_f}{Y_m + Y_f} \, \epsilon_{yh} \right] + \eta_{ff}, \qquad (2.32)$$

and

$$\frac{w_f}{H_m} \frac{\partial H_m}{\partial w_f} = \frac{\gamma_m}{\xi_m} \left[\gamma_f \, \epsilon_{hh} + \frac{w_f L_f}{Y_m + Y_f} \, \epsilon_{yh} \right] + \eta_{fm}, \qquad (2.33)$$

where $\epsilon_{hh} \leq 0$ denotes again the elasticity of H_{mf} to its 'price' w_{mf}, and $\epsilon_{hi} > 0$ the cross-elasticity of I_{mf} to w_{mf}, holding the final product X_{mf} constant, while $\eta_{ij} \leq 0$ represents the elasticity of H_j to w_j, and $\eta_{jk} \geq 0$ the cross-elasticity of H_k to w_j, holding the intermediate product H_{mf} constant $(j,k = m,f)$.

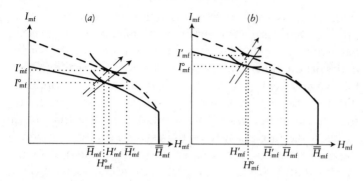

F IG. 2.12

If the time constraint (2.2) is not binding on j, the elasticity of w_{mf} to w_j, γ_j, is equal to the elasticity of H_{mf} to H_j, and thus to the share of the cost of H_{mf} attributable to j, ξ_j. If, on the other hand, H_j is equal to T, j's proportional contribution to the family full income is equal to zero. Suppose, then, that γ_f is greater than γ_m (and thus η_{ff} more negative than η_{mm})—in other words, that the isoquants of $G^{mf}(\ )$ look like the one in Fig. 2.8(b). Suppose, also, that w_f is no greater than w_m. Then, (2.29) and (2.32) tell us that her own-wage elasticity of home-time is more negative than his. Similarly, (2.30) and (2.33) tell us that his cross-wage elasticity of home-time is more positive than hers, and (2.28) and (2.31) that her wage elasticity of commodity demand is more positive than his.

These results[6] have an intuitive explanation. As the wage rate of either partner rises, the intermediate product (joint home-time) becomes more costly and is thus substituted with commodities in the domestic production of the final good. At the same time, the increase in full income associated with the wage rise has a positive effect on the demand for the final good that offsets, to some extent, the negative substitution effect on the derived demand for the intermediate product. However, a rise in her wage rate raises the cost of the intermediate product more, and the full income less, than a rise in his wage rate, because more of her time

than of his is used in the production of the intermediate
product (and less in raising income). Furthermore, a rise in
her wage rate will cause her time to be substituted for his
in the production of the intermediate product, while a rise in
his wage rate will cause a substitution in the opposite
direction. But, as can be inferred quite clearly from Fig. 2.8(b),
the effects of her wage rate are larger in size than those
of his wage rate because of the asymmetric way in which
the two partners' times enter into the production of the
intermediate product. Summing all these effects, it becomes
clear why the home-times of *both* partners, and the demand
for commodities, are more sensitive to changes in the wife's
than in the husband's wage rate.

A number of important implications flow from these
theoretical predictions. One is that, if married women have
a comparative advantage in home-production (in the precise
sense specified above, that they are better at domestic
activities, and no better at market activities) over their
husbands, then their labour supply will rise proportionately
more in response to a rise in female wage rates, than the
labour supply of their husbands would in response to a rise
in male wage rates. Furthermore, the labour supply of the
family as a whole will be more responsive to changes in
female than in male wage rates. Such a phenomenon is well
documented,[7] suggesting that the comparative advantage in
question—whatever its causes—does exist.

The elasticity differential helps to explain why the gradual
rise of female wage rates towards equality with male wage
rates in industrialized countries has brought with it such a
drastic narrowing of the gap between male and female
labour-market participation rates.[8] It also helps to explain
the very rapid diffusion of convenience foods and domestic
time-saving appliances, and the sharp fall in time-consuming
activities, such as having children, since the Second World
War. Yet another implication is that a government interested
in maximizing tax revenues (or minimizing the distortionary
consequences of any desired level of tax revenue) should

tax married men's earnings more heavily than married women's.[9] Fiscal practices such as 'income-splitting', whereby each spouse's taxable income is equal to half the couple's joint income, should therefore be avoided. On the other hand, however, if married women's marginal tax rates were reduced, that would be equivalent to a rise in female wage rates and thus accentuate the move away from time-intensive activities like child-raising—which, in some circumstances, might be undesirable. We shall come back to these issues later on.

2.5. *Transaction Costs*

Up to this point, we have ignored the fact that human transactions have a cost—in time and other resources—and that, the more complex the transaction, the higher its cost. This is relevant to our discussion of home-production arrangements:[10] when two (or more) persons get together to form a joint household, they must expend time and income finding out about each other and negotiating, in the light of that information, a division of tasks and distribution of goods. These initial transaction costs will recur to some extent every time that there is a change in market prices (wages) or more is learned about each other's capabilities. More of these transaction costs arise also from the need to check that each household member contributes to home-production in the agreed manner and does not appropriate more than the agreed share of the output.[11]

All these costs reduce the output and thus the attractiveness of collaborative home-production. A joint household will be formed only if the expected net benefit is greater than the best alternative. This theme will be developed in later chapters, but a related point is worth making now: the long-term nature of the family relationship, which makes it possible to contemplate lengthy production processes such as child-rearing, also reduces the individual incentive to shirk and cheat, and thus transaction costs. A family has thus a double advantage[12] over a non-family household with comparable membership and resources.

The cost of negotiating and policing a complex domestic arrangement may indeed be so high, in a non-family household, as to cancel any efficiency gain arising from division of labour. The only advantage of joining together, in such a case, would then come from the opportunity to share items of expenditure with public-good characteristics, as we shall see in the next chapter.

Transaction costs also help to explain why, in some cases, a household might produce (choose negative inputs of) commodities for the market, alongside goods for its own consumption. According to standard economic theory, there is no advantage in integrating consumption with (commodity) production activities within the same organization —and there is usually a disadvantage, in that the consumption unit, the household, may not be endowed with the mix of work skills needed to produce commodities efficiently. That, however, does not take account of the costs of acquiring information about the personal characteristics and policing the behaviour of workers—costs which may well be lower within a family household than within a commercial firm. Examples of family enterprises successfully competing against specialized commercial organizations are not uncommon, particularly in lines of business requiring personal qualities and work skills that are costly to evaluate without close acquaintance, but not so rare as to be unlikely to be found in the right mix within the same family.[13]

NOTES

1. See Becker (1965), Muth (1966). An influential parallel development is Kelvin Lancaster's 'characteristics approach', whereby the household is seen as mixing commodities with utility-yielding charac-

teristics to achieve the desired balance; see Lancaster (1966). The particular model used in this chapter was first presented in Cigno (1990*a*).

2. Becker and disciples actually talk of market 'goods' and domestically produced 'commodities'. We prefer the more traditional usage of 'good' for something that yields direct utility (and which, as in the case of public goods, may not have a market), and of 'commodity' for something that can be bought or sold in the market.

3. There is an implicit assumption here that none of the commodities bought from the markets are durable (i.e. that households never buy houses, only rent them, and that they go round to the launderette instead of buying washing machines).

4. Notice, however, that we cannot say whether f will actually do the same as m (i.e. participate in the labour market) after the merger. That is because the time of the two partners is assumed, here, to be perfectly homogeneous, so that the allocation of total market-time and total home-time between the two partners is indeterminate.

5. This is also a way of formalizing Becker's contention that the efficiency gain from marriage is due to 'complementarity of traits' between the spouses; see Becker (1973, 1974, 1981).

6. First presented in Cigno (1990*a*).

7. See, for example, Mincer (1962, 1985) and several of the papers in Cain and Watts (1973).

8. In the UK, for example, the female/male wage ratio rose from around 60 per cent in 1960 to just about 70 per cent in 1980, while the ratio of the participation rates rose from under half to over two-thirds.

9. See Boskin and Sheshinski (1983).

10. The discussion that follows draws on Ben-Porath (1980) and Pollak (1985).

11. Becker (1974, 1981) argues that in a family such antisocial behaviour will not arise so long as at least one member is altruistic (i.e. so long as someone's utility increases with the utility of every other member). But, as Manser and Brown (1980) point out, this is the case only if the altruist takes all the decisions, i.e. only if the family is run by an altruistic patriarch (or matriarch) with dictatorial powers.

12. We shall later argue, in Chap. 5, that a long-term mutual commitment enhances productivity in yet another way, by inducing home-specific investments.

13. These points are made in Pollak (1985).

3

Household Size

Economies (diseconomies) of scale, or increasing (decreasing) returns to scale, are usually modelled by directly postulating a cost function concave (convex) in output, or a production function convex (concave) in any linear combination of inputs. That, however, does not explain the phenomenon, merely describes it. In the following discussion of how the size of the household affects the efficiency of its operations, we prefer to retain the natural assumption that the home-production function is linear-homogeneous, and to examine various possible sources of economies or diseconomies explicitly. Since children are part of the output of the home-production process, household size will be measured by the number of adult members only.

3.1. *Division of Labour*

One source of increasing returns to household size we have already encountered in the last chapter, where we found that two non-identical individuals can, through division of labour, generate more goods jointly in a two-person house-hold than they could separately in two one-person house-holds. And the argument does not stop at two. Home-time being an amalgam of separate domestic tasks (shopping, cooking, cleaning, etc.), there may be further efficiency gains to be made by extending the principle of division of labour to the allocation of these specific tasks. Indeed, there is some evidence that this kind of specialization is a prominent feature of domestic organization.[1] Since the scope for assigning different domestic tasks to different members is obviously greater in larger households, it is also clear that the potential for improving efficiency through division of labour increases with the size of the household.

Increasing returns associated with division of labour are further enhanced if the range of home-production possibilities widens with household size. We have already argued, also in the last chapter, that a nuclear-family household is more efficient not only than the one-person households it replaces, but also than any comparable two-person non-family household. By similar arguments, an extended-family household (with grandparents, uncles, and aunts) is more efficient than any sorting of its members into smaller units, and more efficient also than any comparable non-family household of the same size, because it offers more scope for division of labour and opens up more production possibilities. For example, in an extended-family household it may be possible to substitute retired grandparents for parents of employment age in the care of children, thereby generating extra income and, if the grandparents regard the association with their grandchildren as a good, extra home-production possibilities.

3.2. Cost-Sharing

Another possible advantage of a large household is that its members may be able to share and thus reduce the per-capita cost of items of expenditure with 'public good' characteristics, such as furniture, domestic appliances, and living space. In order to separate these kinds of scale economies from those made possible by division of labour and expanding production possibilities, we shall now suppose that all actual and potential household members are identical, and that the home-production technology does not vary with household size.

We can then dispense with subscripts, and write I for the effective per-capita input of commodities, H for per-capita home-time and $X = F(H,I)$ for per-capita output. The number of household members will be denoted by N. In general, the total amount spent by the household to buy commodities will not be NI, but

$$E = N^\gamma I, \qquad 0 < \gamma \leq 1, \qquad (3.1)$$

where γ may be interpreted as a *congestion* parameter: the smaller γ, the greater the scope for cost-sharing. If γ equals unity, it means that all the commodities bought by the household are 'pure private goods'. If γ equalled zero, they would be all 'pure public goods', but we are ruling that out as highly improbable.

Now, let $C(X,N,w)$ denote the least cost of producing X units of goods per head, in a household with N members, given that the wage rate is w. As this cost function is obtained by choosing H and I to minimize $(Hw + IN^{\gamma-1})$, the effect on C of a small change[2] in N is given, according to the Envelope Theorem, by

$$C_N = -(1-\gamma)IN^{\gamma-2}, \qquad (3.2)$$

which is clearly non-positive and non-decreasing in N for the restrictions imposed on the value of γ. As N increases, per-capita costs will thus either remain constant or, if there is scope for cost-sharing ($\gamma < 1$), decrease. In the absence of other considerations, the efficient household size would thus be either indeterminate or infinitely large.[3]

A reason why, in reality, households do not expand without bound could be that per-capita transaction costs rise with N. Indeed, since any organization grows in complexity and becomes more difficult to manage as it gets bigger, that seems a very likely explanation. Suppose, for example, that per-capita transaction costs increase with N by a factor of t. The sum of production and transaction costs per head will then be minimized where

$$-C_N = t. \qquad (3.3)$$

As the left-hand side of this equation is non-increasing in N, households enjoying lower t will thus tend to be larger (see

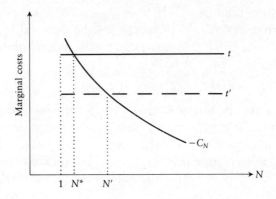

FIG. 3.1

Fig. 3.1). In particular, family households will be larger than comparable non-family households for the reasons discussed in the last chapter.

We can also see how the wage rate affects household size according to this approach. The opportunity cost of H,

$$w^* \equiv \frac{F_H}{F_I} = wN^{1-\gamma}, \tag{3.4}$$

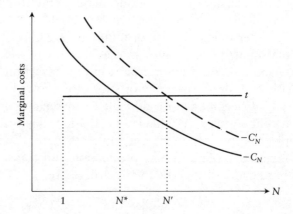

FIG. 3.2

increases with the wage rate. As w rises, I is substituted for H in the production of X. Consequently, $-C_N$ shifts upwards and the efficient household becomes larger (see Fig. 3.2).

3.3. *The Value of Privacy*

An alternative approach to the determination of household size[4] is to postulate that the happiness or *utility* of each household member, denoted by U, depends on N, as well as on X,

$$U = U(X,N). \tag{3.5}$$

In other words, the presence of other people in the same household affects utility directly, as well as indirectly through its influence on X. Assuming that N is a good only up to a certain household size N^0, beyond which companionship turns into an intrusion on privacy, U_N will be positive for N smaller than B^0, and negative for N larger.

Maximizing (3.5) subject to the per-capita budget constraint

$$C(X,N,w) = V + wT \equiv Y \tag{3.6}$$

requires the marginal rate of substitution of X for N (the negative of each member's marginal valuation of privacy in terms of other goods) to equal the ratio of their marginal costs (i.e. the negative of the opportunity cost of privacy in terms of other goods),

$$\frac{U_N}{U_X} = \frac{C_N}{C_X}. \tag{3.7}$$

As illustrated in Fig. 3.3(a), if there is no scope for cost-sharing ($\gamma = 1$), the opportunity cost of privacy is zero and there is thus nothing to be gained from increasing N beyond the point where it ceases to be a good. If, however, there is scope for cost-sharing ($\gamma < 1$) and it is thus possible to increase X by increasing N, it is then worth trading some privacy for other goods, as illustrated in Fig. 3.3(b).

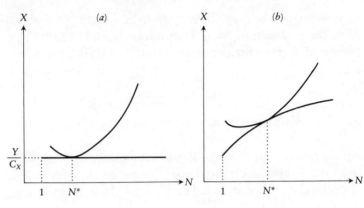

FIG. 3.3

On the face of it, this approach does not tell us anything different from that examined in the last section: all it does is to measure transaction costs directly in terms of utility instead of commodities. Consider, however, the effect of a wage rise. Assuming that the household supplies some labour to the market ($H < T$), full income Y will then rise. If γ is unity, that will have no effect on N (see Fig. 3.4(a)). For γ less than unity, however, the opportunity cost of privacy may rise or fall, depending on whether the marginal cost of privacy ($-C_N$) or that of other goods (C_X) increases more as the wage rate rises.[5]

If the opportunity cost of privacy falls as the wage rate rises, that will have a negative substitution effect on N. Since the household size (with $\gamma < 1$) will be such that N is regarded as a 'bad', there will also be a negative full-income effect. As illustrated in Fig. 3.4(b), household size will then definitely fall. If, on the other hand, the opportunity cost of privacy rises, then full-income and substitution effects will have the opposite sign. The net result of a wage rise may in that case be a fall in N,[6] as illustrated in Fig. 3.4(c), but a rise is also possible.

In contrast with the cost-minimizing model's prediction that household size increases with the wage rate, the utility-maximizing approach thus shows that household size may be inversely related to the wage rate (or independent of it if there is no scope for domestic cost-sharing). According to this line of reasoning, higher wage earners would thus be expected to live in smaller households (perhaps of only one), and a generalized wage rise could be expected to lower the average household size. That is indeed borne out by the empirical evidence,[7] from which it may be inferred that cost-sharing is a consideration in household formation and, furthermore, that people regard privacy as a substitute for other goods. While useful in comparing households of given size, the transactions-cost approach is thus inadequate for the determination of household size.

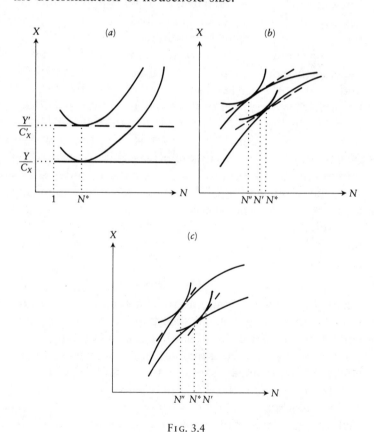

FIG. 3.4

3.4. *Commuting Costs*

Another consideration restricting the size of a household
may be that the per-capita cost of delivering the services of
its members to spatially distributed labour markets increases
with household size. If employment (including self-employ-
ment) opportunities are widely scattered over the territory,
it is in fact obvious that the costs of commuting to work
could be reduced by matching the geographical pattern of
habitation as closely as possible to that of employment, and
also that the smaller the households, the closer the match.
The same may be true even if employment opportunities are
concentrated at a small number of locations, provided that
the mix of employment opportunities for individuals with
different characteristics is not the same at each location.

Let us then define $T(pN)$ as the minimum cost of travel to
and from work, per head of a population of fixed size P,
given that each member of this population lives in a household of size N $(1 \leqslant N \leqslant P)$, and that the rate of labour
market participation is p $(0 < p \leqslant 1)$. The function $T(\ )$
assigns to each household size a per-capita cost of travel
minimized with respect to locational pattern, and it is thus
constructed by finding, for each N, the cost-minimizing
locations of (P/N) households.[8]

Assuming cost-sharing $(\gamma < 1)$, the household size that
minimizes the sum of home-production and travel costs
satisfies

$$- C_N = pT'(pN), \tag{3.8}$$

where $T'(pN)$ is the marginal transport cost, positive and
typically increasing in N. As shown in Fig. 3.5, commuting
costs thus condition household size in a way similar to
transaction costs. The difference lies, once again, in the
effect of wage changes. Suppose, for example, that w rises.
As we already know, the $- C_N$ curve will then shift upwards.
At the same time, however, it is likely that p will rise (i.e.
that a larger number of people will go out to work, or the

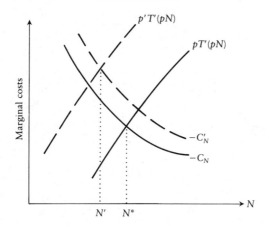

same number work more days).[9] Therefore, the graph of pT' is likely to shift upwards too. Depending on the relative size of these two effects, the cost-minimizing household size may then rise or, as in Fig. 3.5, fall in response to the wage increase.

Travel costs can be incorporated into the utility-maximizing model of the last section by adding $T(pN)$ to the left-hand side of the budget equation (3.6). An optimum will then satisfy

$$\frac{U_N}{U_X} = \frac{C_N + pT'\ (pN)}{C_X}.$$ (3.9)

As in the last section, the marginal value of privacy in terms of commodities is thus equated to the opportunity cost. Here, however, this cost is reduced by the marginal transport cost of N. As illustrated in Fig. 3.6, drawn under the assumption that the cost-minimizing N is finite and greater than unity, this carries the implication that, at an optimum, N could still be regarded by household members as a good rather than a 'bad'. That is so because the budget curve is now upward-sloping to the left, and downward-sloping to the right, of the cost-minimizing household size, denoted by

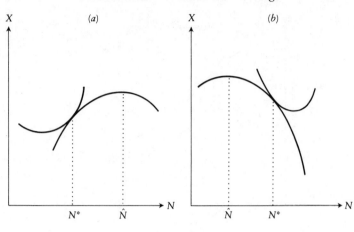

FIG. 3.6

$\hat{N}$, which is the point where the diseconomies associated with commuting are just offset by the economies deriving from domestic cost-sharing. If preferences and market conditions are such, that the optimal household size, N^*, is smaller than $\hat{N}$, as in panel (a), the opportunity cost of privacy is positive at the optimum. In that case, as in the model of Section 3.3, the accession of another person to an optimally sized household would be regarded by its members as an intrusion on privacy, a source of disutility. Conditions could be such, however, that N^* is larger than $\hat{N}$, as in panel (b). In that case, people actually prefer to live in larger households. What is stopping them is that the opportunity cost of privacy is negative (the extra commuting costs would more than compensate for domestic savings) and larger, in absolute terms, than the value placed on the extra companionship.

In the case where N^* is less than $\hat{N}$, the analysis of the effect of a wage rate change is similar to that of the last section. A wage rise will definitely reduce household size if the opportunity cost of privacy is decreasing in w, but not otherwise. The situation is reversed, however, if N^* is larger than $\hat{N}$, because the number of household members is then regarded as a good and, therefore, w has a positive full-income effect on household size. In that case, a wage rise will definitely increase household size if the opportunity cost of privacy is increasing in w, but not otherwise.

Since, under present assumptions, the opportunity cost of privacy is given by $[-(C_N + pT')/C_X]$, rather than just $(-C_N/C_X)$ as in the last section, there is now a greater chance that this cost will decrease as w increases. The evidence, mentioned earlier, of an inverse relationship between wage rates and household size could thus be taken as an indication that the optimal household size is smaller than cost considerations alone would dictate—in other words, that communal living is generally disliked. We shall see in Chapters 7 and 9, however, that there are other ways, not incompatible with our present arguments, of explaining the empirical regularity in question.

NOTES

1. In their major survey of New York State households, Walker and Woods (1976) found a high degree of specialization in the allocation of home-time among various domestic tasks, even where division of labour between home and market work was not much in evidence.
2. Here the integer problem rears its ugly head: N can only be 1, 2, 3, etc. As with any other indivisible object (even drinks are sold in indivisible units) we seek to approximate the effect of a finite change with that of an infinitesimal one.
3. If we bring back into the picture scale economies associated with division of labour and expanding production possibilities, the efficient size is infinite even without cost-sharing.
4. The analysis that follows is inspired by Ermisch (1981b). The specific model used here was first presented in Cigno (1990a).
5. The opportunity cost of privacy rises with w if the elasticity of substitution of commodities for time in the domestic production of goods is unity and unearned income is zero, but it falls for various combinations of small elasticity and large property.
6. That is indeed the most likely outcome if the reason why the opportunity cost of privacy has risen with w is that V is low (see n. 5), for in

such a case L would be large, and the full-income effect would thus be likely to dominate the substitution effect.

7. Ermisch (1981*b*) estimates the wage and the income elasticity of household size in the UK at -0.3, and -0.2, respectively. While there is no other direct evidence on wage elasticity, Hickman (1974) reports an income elasticity of household size in the USA very similar to Ermisch's, suggesting that the wage elasticity too may be of the order estimated for the UK. Furthermore, Borsch-Supan (1986) and Ermisch (1987*a*) estimate strongly negative effects of housing prices on the demand for individual accommodation. This is consistent with the theory and, since housing accounts for a large proportion (20–5 per cent in the USA and UK) of household expenditure, provides additional indirect evidence of negative wage elasticity.

8. Cigno (1971) constructs such a function for processing plants that collect raw materials from widely scattered sources and deliver output to a multiplicity of spatially separated outlets.

9. Particularly if female wage rates rise; see Sec. 2.4.

4

The Marriage Market

In the last two chapters we examined some good reasons why two or more people might be more efficient in the use of their resources if they lived together than if they lived apart, but whether a named individual would be actually better off associating with another named individual may depend on how any efficiency gain resulting from the union is shared out between them.[1] Indeed, it does depend on the distribution of home-produced goods among members of the household in all cases where at least some of those goods can be individually appropriated (i.e. wherever the output of home-production does not consist entirely of 'pure' public goods).

In the present chapter we examine how these considerations affect the choice of marriage partner under the assumption that the only available forms of household organization are the one-person household and the nuclear family, but much of what we shall have to say applies just as well to the choice of partners in any other kind of multi-person household. Also, in what follows we assume that pure altruism does not play a significant role in the choice of marriage (or any other) partner. We assume, in other words, that each person is out to secure the best possible arrangement for himself or herself, and cares about the partner's welfare only to the extent that it conditions his or her own. That need not remain true, however, once the family is formed, and typically does not apply to the relationship, examined in later chapters, between parents and children.

4.1. *An Extended Marriage Game*

If each person derives satisfaction only from his or her own consumption of home-produced goods, maximizing the utility of any person j is then the same as maximizing the quantity of goods C_j allotted to j. Clearly, C_j will be identical with X_j, and thus depend only on j's personal characteristics, if he or she is single. Otherwise, it will depend also on whom j marries and on how the home-product is divided.

We are thus back to the marriage game discussed in Chapter 1, with the added complication that each player's preference ranking of potential partners is no longer given a priori, but is itself dependent on the deal that he or she is able to extract from each member of the opposite sex.[2] The sorting of players into couples and singles must then be determined simultaneously with the distribution of the benefits of each marriage—a situation not unlike a market, where buyers are matched with sellers by the same process which determines the price and, consequently, the share of the gain to each party in the transaction.

The core of this extended game is still defined as the set of all feasible allocations that cannot be blocked by any single player or couple of players (of opposite sex). However, an allocation must now specify not only who marries whom, but also who gets what out of the deal. Let us then denote by X_j^* the quantity of goods that j could produce efficiently on his or her own (i.e. the maximum X_j, subject to j's one-person budget constraint) and by X_{mf}^* the quantity that a male, m, and a female, f, could efficiently produce together. For an allocation to be feasible, it must be true that

$$C_j \leq X_j^* \quad \text{for any unmarried j} \qquad (4.1)$$

and

$$C_m + C_f \leq X_{mf}^* \quad \text{for any married couple (m,f).} \quad (4.2)$$

Clearly, any core allocation must give each j, married or not, at least his or her single's output,

$$C_j \geq X_j^* \quad \text{for all j,} \qquad (4.3)$$

with the equality sign holding, in view of (4.1), if j actually is single. Similarly, the quantities assigned to the members of any potential couple (m,f) must add up to no less than their potential married output,

$$C_m + C_f \geq X_{mf}^* \quad \text{for all m and f,} \qquad (4.4)$$

with the equality sign holding, in view of (4.2), if m and f actually are married to each other.

There may be several allocations in the core, some characterized by the same sorting of players into couples and singles, some not. But, any core sorting will have the property that the sum total of the quantities of goods produced by all couples and singles is at a maximum—otherwise it would always be possible for at least one individual or potential couple to produce more than he, she, or they have been allocated, and thus block the allocation. Hence,

$$\Sigma_j C_j = \max C(S), \qquad (4.5)$$

where $C(S)$ denotes the sum total of the quantities that could be efficiently produced by all the participants in the game if the sorting were S.

Suppose, for example, that there are only two men ($m = m_1, m_2$) and two women ($f = f_1, f_2$). Suppose, also, that the quantities each individual and each potential couple can produce are as shown in the following output matrix:

	f_1	f_2	
m_1	10	4	2
m_2	4	10	1
	1	2	

(4.6)

The (m,f) cell shows the quantity of goods that m and f could produce if married to each other, while the last element of row m shows the quantity that m could produce on his own, and the last element of column f shows the amount that f could produce on her own.

In this example, total output is maximized by the sorting (m_1f_1,m_2f_2), according to which m_1 marries f_1, and m_2 marries f_2, thereby producing in all

$$C(m_1f_1,m_2f_2) = 20. \tag{4.7}$$

The maximum, in this case, is unique (all other possible sortings produce less), but there are many unblockable ways of distributing the total among the participants.

One of the core allocations is

$$A_1(m_1f_1,m_2f_2) = \begin{bmatrix} 3,7 & \vdots \\ & 7,3 \vdots \\ \text{------} \vdots \text{--} \end{bmatrix} \tag{4.8}$$

where the first entry in cell (m,f) is the quantity allocated to m and the second is the quantity allocated to f, so that m_1 receives 3 units of output, f_1 receives 7, etc. A_1 cannot be blocked by m_1 remaining single because, on his own, he could produce only 2. Nor could it be blocked by m_1 marrying f_2 instead of f_1 because, as a couple, m_1 and f_2 could produce only 4, while the sum of the quantities assigned to them in $A_1(m_1f_1,m_2f_2)$ is 6. Similar considerations would dissuade f_1, f_2, or m_2 from remaining single, and m_2 from marrying f_1.

Another core allocation is

$$A_2(m_1f_1,m_2f_2) = \begin{bmatrix} 7,3 & \vdots \\ & 3,7 \vdots \\ \text{------} \vdots \text{--} \end{bmatrix} \tag{4.9}$$

Indeed, any distribution of 20 units of output which gives at least 2 to each player is in the core.

4.2. *Assortative Mating?*

In the last example, neither member of either sex could be said to be superior to the other. But, suppose that the output matrix was:

$$
\begin{array}{c|cc|c}
 & f_1 & f_2 & \\
\hline
m_1 & 10 \quad 5 & & 2 \\
m_2 & 9 \quad 2 & & 1 \\
\hline
 & 2 \quad 1 & & \\
\end{array}
\qquad (4.10)
$$

Here m_1 is clearly superior to m_2 because, whether or not he marries and whomever he marries, he is more efficient than m_2. Similarly, f_1 is superior to f_2. Will the superior man marry the superior woman?

Clearly not, because, if m_1 married f_1 and m_2 married f_2, the total output

$$C(m_1f_1, m_2f_2) = 12 \qquad (4.11)$$

would be less than if m_1 married f_2 and m_2 married f_1,

$$C(m_2f_2, m_2f_1) = 14. \qquad (4.12)$$

Hence, no matter how good a deal f_1 offered m_1, f_2 could always outbid her. Similarly, m_2 could always offer f_1 more than m_1 would.

As it happens, the output-maximizing sorting (m_1f_2, m_2f_1) is again unique, and there are again many unblockable ways of distributing the total, including

$$
A_1(m_1f_2, m_2f_1) =
\begin{bmatrix}
 & 3,2 & \\
\underline{1,8} & & \\
\end{bmatrix}
\qquad (4.13)
$$

and

$$A_2(m_1f_2, m_2f_1) = \begin{bmatrix} & & 4,11 \\ & 2,7 & \\ \hline \end{bmatrix} \qquad (4.14)$$

Notice that the superior man gets a better deal in A_2, while the superior woman gets a better deal in A_1, but in each case both do better marrying the inferior member of the opposite sex than they would otherwise.

As anticipated in Chapter 1, assortative mating is thus *not* the norm:[3] since shares can be unequal, maximizing one's share of the product of one's marriage need not entail choosing the partner who maximizes that product (it does in (4.6), but not in (4.10)). The answer to the question 'What did she (he) ever see in him (her)?' that springs to mind at the sight of an obviously uneven match is thus: 'He (she) gives her (him) more than anyone else would.'

Notice, finally, that these predictions are valid only to the extent that the spouses can individually appropriate the benefits of their marriage. Had we assumed that the output of marriage consists entirely of pure public goods, so that one spouse's enjoyment of it does not diminish the other's, superman would have made off with superwoman leaving the lesser man and woman to each other. In that case, the marriage game would have been inefficient, in the sense that total output and consumption would not have been the largest possible.[4]

4.3. *Who Will Be Single?*

If one sex outnumbers the other, someone will obviously remain single, but those left without a partner will not necessarily be the ones who have less to contribute to married life. Suppose, for example, that there are three men,

m_1, m_2, and m_3, but only two women, f_1 and f_2. If the output matrix is

	f_1	f_2	
m_1	10	5	3
m_2	9	2	1
m_3	2	5	1
	2	1	

$$(4.15)$$

the maximum total output is

$$C(m_1, m_2f_1, m_3f_2) = 17. \qquad (4.16)$$

The reader can easily check that m_1 will stay single, even though he is best all round, simply because neither of the women will be willing to offer him at least his single's output.

Indeed, some people might remain single even if numbers are equal. For example, if there were two men and two women, and the output matrix were

	f_1	f_2	
m_1	10	5	2
m_2	9	2	2
	2	2	

$$(4.17)$$

there would then be two efficient sortings: (m_1f_2, m_2f_1) according to which everyone gets married, and (m_1f_1, m_2, f_2) according to which m_2 and f_2 do not. In general, all we can say is that, the more a person is capable of producing goods on his or her own, the more, other things being equal, he or she will get out of any marriage deal, but the less likely it is that such a deal will be on offer.

Factors which increase the productivities of singles (the marginal entries in our output matrices) relative to that of couples (entries in the body of the output matrices) are thus likely to reduce the incidence of marriage. That would be true, in particular, of a rise in the wage rates of women relative to those of men, because it would reduce the extent of domestic division of labour, and thus increase the output of single women more than that of couples. Empirical evidence from the USA and the UK supports this theoretical proposition.[5]

By contrast, any change of tax regime in favour of married couples would increase, other things being equal, the incidence of marriage. Not to the same extent, however, if the regime change lowered the marginal rate of tax on married women's earnings—as, for example, with 'tax splitting', already mentioned in Section 2.4—because that would increase the incentive for married women to go out to work, and thus reduce the gain from domestic division of labour.

4.4. *Competitive Distributions*

We have seen that, even in cases where the efficient sorting happens to be unique, the core of the marriage game may still contain many different allocations, distinguished by the way in which the product is distributed. A pattern of distribution that has received special attention in the economics of the family literature is the one where each person, married or unmarried, is 'paid' the marginal product (in home-produced goods) of his or her home-time and income,

$$C_j = F_H G_j^{\mathrm{mf}} H_j + F_I[w_j(T - H_j) + V_j]. \qquad (4.18)$$

Given the analogy between this way of distributing home-produced goods and the way in which commercially produced commodities are distributed among owners of productive factors in a system of perfectly competitive product and factor markets, we shall call this a *competitive distribution*.

In the absence of cost-sharing, any such distribution would exactly exhaust the output, and thus be feasible. Furthermore, it would be unblockable because, for any married couple (m,f),

$$X^*_{mf} = (H_m G_m + H_f G_f)F_H + I_{mf}F_I, \qquad (4.19)$$

so that, given (4.18),

$$X^*_{mf} = C_m + C_f. \qquad (4.20)$$

Similarly, for any single j,

$$X^*_j = H_j F_H + I_j F_I = C_j. \qquad (4.21)$$

An attraction of such a distribution is that it is 'fair', in the sense that what one gets depends strictly on what one has to offer (but is it fair that some have so much more to offer than others?). Notice, also, that if j spends any time at all working for a wage, then the shadow-wage rate $(F_H G_j^{mf}/F_I)$ will be equal to the wage rate w_j, and C_j will thus be the equivalent, in home-produced goods, of j's full income,

$$C_j = (w_j T + V_j)F_I \equiv Y_j F_I \text{ for } H_j < T. \quad (4.18')$$

Another attraction of competitive allocations is that they make it easy to predict the distributional implications of differences between individuals. For example, out of two persons differing in their earning ability, but otherwise identical, the one who commands the higher wage rate in the labour market will also get the better deal in the marriage market; similarly, the wealthier of the two will get the better marriage deal if they differ only in the amount of property owned.

In general, the core of the marriage game may contain other types of distribution, with just as much chance of being implemented as a competitive one. Suppose, however, that there is more than one person of each type. Suppose, for example, that there are two m_1-type males. The room for manœuvre available to each of these characters in making deals with potential marriage partners is then restricted by the fact that both must obtain the same deal, otherwise the less well-treated m_1 could undercut the one who comes off better. If there were more than two m_1s, the bargaining power of each of them would be further reduced. At the limit, if there were a very large number (strictly speaking, an infinite number) of each type of potential marriage partners, nobody would have any bargaining power, and each person would have to accept the 'going rate' like a price-taker in a perfectly competitive market. Indeed, it is a standard result in economic theory that the core of a 'large' game admits only competitive allocations.

But, how realistic is it to talk of large numbers of identical individuals? Even within a conventional commodity or labour market context it is hard to think of two—let alone many—traders having exactly the same characteristics. All the more so if we are talking of potential marriage partners! None the less, the competitive market model is regarded by some authors[6] as a good enough approximation to reality for densely populated areas, where each person has many close substitutes, and any woman (man) may thus refuse a marriage deal that appears to be out of line with the norm for someone with her (his) attractions, in the confident expectation that there are 'plenty more where he (she) came from'.

4.5. *Search Costs*

We must now raise again the question of how equilibrium (i.e., in general, a core allocation) is reached in the marriage market. The answer we gave at the end of Chapter 1— namely that people go on searching for a partner until an unblockable allocation comes about—is inadequate, now that the desirability of a match has been seen to depend on a comparison of costs and benefits, because search itself may be costly and thus reduce the benefit of any match that might result from it.

The cost of searching for a marriage partner consists of the utility forgone as time and expenditure are diverted from home-production to sampling the opposite sex, net of any utility that the searcher might derive from the search itself. The benefit consists of the extra utility that the searcher hopes to gain from a new domestic arrangement. If marriage is indissoluble, or the cost of dissolving it is prohibitively high, the only persons searching for a partner will be singles. Otherwise, some married people also will participate in the search.

An individual will stop searching when the marginal cost of search (the utility of the home-produced goods forgone by courting yet another member of the opposite sex, minus any utility derived from so doing) equals the marginal benefit (the improvement on either the present situation or the last offer received, whichever is better, expected from courting another person).[7] So long as the marginal cost is positive for at least some of the participants in the marriage game, it is possible, indeed likely, that some will stop searching *before* a core allocation has been achieved and, therefore, that there will be some degree of mismatch.

The costs and benefits of search, and thus the duration of search, depend on the personal characteristics of the searcher and of everyone else in the market. Given the latter, we may thus expect individuals with low search costs to search longer. Indeed, the incidence of confirmed bachelors and spinsters—i.e. of people who have given up the search before finding a mate—is typically higher in rural areas with scattered settlements, where the material cost of search is relatively high, than in densely populated districts. By contrast, philanderers may be described as people whose search costs are very low (perhaps even negative) because they derive so much pleasure from the sampling process itself.

Other things being equal, the longer the search, the better

the match at the end of it. Therefore, individuals with lower search costs may be expected to find 'better' mates. An econometric study of marriage patterns in the Philippines indeed shows that the quality of the husband, as measured by expected earnings at the date of marriage, is positively related to the number of years that the wife has spent searching,[8] and inversely related to the cost of her search (as measured by population dispersion and female to male sex ratio). Similarly, there is evidence that in the UK[9] and elsewhere the risk of marriage failure (a measure of the degree of mismatch) is higher for women who marry younger (search less).

NOTES

1. Equidistribution was implicitly assumed in the last chapter, but that was only because all potential household members were assumed to be the same. In general, there is no a priori reason why different household members, making unequal contributions to home-production, should receive equal rewards.

2. The approach followed in this section is due to Becker (1973, 1974, 1981).

3. In much of the economics literature, the expression 'assortative mating' is used, more narrowly, to indicate marriage between individuals who share *some* characteristics, rather than marriage between similarly attractive individuals. In particular, it is argued in Becker (1973, 1981) that individuals look for a spouse with 'complementary traits', meaning by that personal characteristics which increase X_{mf} more than they increase the sum of X_m and X_f. This leads, in Becker's terminology, to *negative* assortative mating, e.g. to high-wage men marrying low-wage women. Boulier and Rosenzweig (1984) report evidence of negative assortative mating with respect to level of education in the Philippines. However, since a person is characterized by a great variety of traits, it seems misleading to talk of spouses being (positively or negatively) assorted on the basis of just one or few of these traits. We prefer, therefore, not to talk of assortative mating in this narrower sense.

4. That, of course, is true also of conventional commodity markets.

5. Empirically, a fall in the male/female wage differential reduces the incidence of marriage primarily by raising the age of marriage, but it reduces also the number of those who marry at all; see Keeley (1979) and Ermisch (1981a).
6. For example, Becker (1973, 1981), Freiden (1974), Grossbard-Shechtman (1984).
7. See Keeley (1977) for a fuller analysis.
8. Each additional year a woman waits before getting married in the Philippines is estimated to increase the husband's expected wealth by 16 per cent; see Boulier and Rosenzweig (1984).
9. See Ermisch (1987c).

5

The Marriage Contract

In the last chapter, we gave an economic explanation of why a man and a woman might find it advantageous to marry. It remains to be explained why they should want to restrict their future freedom of choice by entering into a long-term marriage contract. It also remains to be explained why they might favour a public form of contract, which hands over to the State the power to determine whether and on which terms their union can be terminated, as against a purely private one where those terms and conditions are written into the contract by the parties themselves. Indeed, it remains to be explained why the State should want to be involved in such personal matters, and lend its seal of approval to couples who choose to have their relationship thus regulated. To simply say that people marry in church or at the registry office out of religious conviction or fear of social stigma would not explain the incidence of such marriages among non-believers, in societies or strata of society where alternative arrangements hardly raise an eyebrow. Nor would it offer a rational explanation of why many societies discriminate, fiscally and otherwise, in favour of publicly married couples.

5.1. *Specialized Human Capital*

It is widely accepted that the ability to perform an activity increases, in general, with the amount of time dedicated to that activity: practice makes perfect. A way of formalizing this idea is via the concept of specialized human capital.[1]

Suppose, for example, that j's wage rate, w_j, is determined by

$$w_j = \omega \, k_j, \qquad (5.1)$$

where k_j is a stock of market-specific human capital embodying j's earning skills, and ω is the market rate of return to such an asset. Suppose, also, that this type of human capital increases with work experience,

$$k_j = k_0 + \beta L_j, \; \beta > 0. \qquad (5.2)$$

The opportunity cost of j's home-time is, in this case, not just the wage rate forgone, w_j, but that plus the wage increase, $\beta \omega L_j$, missed by not participating in the labour market for a unit of time.

The implications are illustrated in Fig. 5.1, where the iso-cost (shown as a broken curve) is now convex to the origin because the ratio of his opportunity cost to hers is decreasing in his home-time and increasing in hers. Both the panels (*a*) and (*b*) are drawn under the assumption that m and f are interchangeable in so far as their domestic role is concerned. In (*a*), the isoquant is more convex than the isocosts (i.e. the marginal rate of technical substitution falls faster than the ratio of the opportunity costs) and it is thus efficient for the spouses to share equally in domestic activities at $(\bar{H},\bar{H})$. In (*b*), the isocosts are more convex than the isoquant and one of the partners, no matter which, must specialize completely

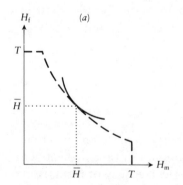
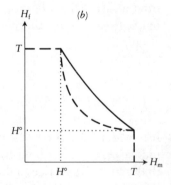

F ɪ ɢ. 5.1

in home-production: the cost of production is the same whether they opt for (T,H^0) or (H^0,T).

Similar arguments can be produced if the opportunities for acquiring new skills are to be found within the home, rather than in the market place. Suppose, for example, that the home-product is a function of each partner's *effective* home-time h_jH_j, where

$$h_j = h_0 + \alpha H_j, \quad \alpha > 0, \qquad (5.3)$$

is the stock of home-specific human capital embodying j's skill in the domestic production of goods. If domestic learning opportunities are sufficiently important (α sufficiently large), the isoquants are in such a case concave to the origin, and only corner solutions can be efficient. In Fig. 5.2, the two partners are assumed to be interchangeable as far as their effective time contribution to home-production is concerned, yet one of them—either of them if their wage rates are equal as in the case illustrated, otherwise the one with the lower wage rate—finds it efficient to specialize completely in domestic activities.

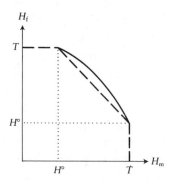

FIG. 5.2

In reality, there will be scope for accumulating specialized human capital both at home and in the labour market, and it is an empirical question whether the first or the second of these phenomena is quantitatively more relevant. Whichever is the case, however, it is important to note that our conclusions so far have been reached under the assumption that the two partners start married life with exactly the same endowments of specialized human capital (k_0 or h_0) and with exactly the same ability to acquire more (β or α). Furthermore, we have seen that complete specialization by one partner can turn out to be beneficial even without asymmetries in the technology of home-production. It is the element of increasing returns created by the accumulation of human capital, rather than any personal predisposition, which makes specialization advantageous. Any, even slight, asymmetry would, however, tip the balance of comparative advantage and decide who specializes in what. For an example of such an asymmetry, we need look no further than the difference between the male and the female role in the production of children.

Unequal endowments of specialized human capital, or unequal aptitudes for learning particular skills have much the same implications as technological asymmetries—and it matters little whether any such disparity is real or just presumed. For example, observing that married women command generally lower wage rates than men, a newly married couple might incorrectly infer that women have inherently lower earning ability. In the light of that, they would then proceed to allocate the woman's time entirely to home-production, thereby allowing the man to acquire more marketable skills and apparently validating their initial misconception. The same observation might also lead parents to spend more on the professional education of their sons than of their daughters, in the mistaken belief that the former yields the higher financial return. As those young men and women would consequently reach marriage with unequal endowments of marketable skills, that would then be reason enough for the latter to specialize in home-production, thereby apparently validating the belief that led to the disparity in the first place. Both these examples suggest that, once established, a pattern of specialization may tend to be self-perpetuating.

5.2. *Benefits of a Private Contract*

Be that as it may, the opportunity to accumulate productivity-enhancing human capital is clearly one of the advantages of marriage. There is a problem, however, in that home-specific human capital is not entirely portable: if a marriage breaks up, any skills pertaining specifically to the married state cease to be of any value until the person who has them remarries, and any which pertain specifically to that marriage vanish anyway. If a union is not expected to last long, therefore, not enough of this type of human capital will be accumulated, and some of the potential gain from the marriage will remain unrealized.

Other assets, too, may depreciate in the event of separation. Among domestically produced assets, the most obvious example is children, who lose some of their public-good characteristics (and, typically, become also more costly to maintain and gain access to) if the parents split up.[2] Examples of purchased assets depreciating with the breakdown of marriage are the marital home and any other durable commodity to which the couple attaches sentimental value while the marriage lasts, but which would not be as highly valued by the market, or by either partner, once the marriage is over. The problem here, as with human capital, is that part of the asset is specific to a particular household and, therefore, that less of it is accumulated if the household in question is not expected to last long.

Another problem arises from the fact that, while home-specific human capital is not entirely portable, market-specific human capital is.[3] In the absence of binding agreements, this asymmetry would, after a while, allow the party who had specialized in market-related activities to make credible threats to break the marriage in order to extract a more favourable deal. As neither party would be inclined to weaken its bargaining position by locking itself into home-specific human capital under such conditions, neither would specialize in home-centred pursuits and not enough of either kind of human capital would be accumulated. There is thus a powerful argument not only for having a long-term contract but also for having one that specifies in advance, before personal characteristics are altered by the process of domestic specialization, how the benefits of marriage are to be shared between the parties.

Another argument to the same effect is that, apart from any bargaining asymmetries, transaction costs are lower if negotiations are carried out in advance. That applies with particular force to the division of family assets in the event of separation, the negotiation of which is more likely to be acrimonious if conducted at the end rather than at the beginning of a marriage. Transaction costs are minimized, according to this argument, if the contract specifies not only how the joint home-product is to be shared while the marriage lasts, but also how any transferable resources are to be allocated between the parties in the event of separation, and what compensatory payments are to be made thereafter in view of the fact that some of the assets (e.g. human capital) cannot be transferred from one person to another.

That, however, is easier said than done because, at the date of marriage, the couple's future is still surrounded by considerable uncertainty. For a start, as pointed out at the end of the last chapter, marriage matches are generally made *before* all possible alternatives have been explored. Hence, at the date of marriage a couple does not know whether and when either or both of them will find a better alternative. Indeed, incomplete premarital search may also mean that neither party is fully informed about the other's personal characteristics—some of which are, in any case, not directly observable and can only be gauged by monitoring actual performance over a long period of time. Besides, market prices are likely to change over married life. For all these reasons, the efficient future allocations of the couple's time and other resources are uncertain at the date when the marriage contract is drawn up.

5.3. *Forms of Private Contract*

Let us examine some of the possible forms a private marriage contract could take.

1. *Contingent contract.* The agreed allocation of time and division of the home-product are made contingent on future information ('if, after a trial period, I turn out to be a splendid houseperson and you God's gift to the stockbroking profession, and provided that prices remain as they are now, I will look after the home, you will dedicate yourself to making money, and each of us will take half the output; if, on the other hand, . . .'). The duration of marriage is also contingent on information: the couple agree to separate if and when both are better off under alternative arrangements, or one gains enough from the separation to be able to compensate the other. As the number of conceivable contingencies is very large, the legal and personal costs of transacting so complex a contract are likely to exceed the expected benefit for most couples.

2. *Fixed-share contract.* The couple agree to keep adjusting their time allocation in response to new information so as to keep X_{mf} at a maximum, but not to change their proportional output entitlements, which are fixed for good at the date of marriage ('I will go out to work or look after the home according to where my comparative advantage lies, but I shall always get three-fifths of our output'). Either party can terminate the contract at any moment without penalty. The implications are shown in fig. 5.3,[4] where s $(0 < s < 1)$ denotes the fixed share of X_{mf} negotiated by m, while A_j stands for the best alternative available to j = m,f. The union will be

efficient if its output turns out to be at least as large as the sum of the best alternatives,

$$X_{mf} \geq A_m + A_f \tag{5.4}$$

(i.e. anywhere on or above the 45° line), but m will want to separate if it turns out that

$$A_m > sX_{mf} \tag{5.5}$$

(areas I, II, and III), and f if

$$A_f > (1 - s)X_{mf} \tag{5.6}$$

(areas I, V, and VI). Therefore, the incidence of separation will be 'too high', in the sense that the couple will split up in situations (represented by the shaded areas III and V) where their union is efficient and both partners would thus be better off staying together if only they could alter their shares of the output. If the initial transaction cost of this type of contract is not very high, the consequences of inefficient separations may not be too serious, because the same parties can remarry on new terms. But, that leaves the door open to opportunistic bargaining, almost as if there were no contract at all, and it thus creates disincentives to the accumulation of specialized human capital as already explained.

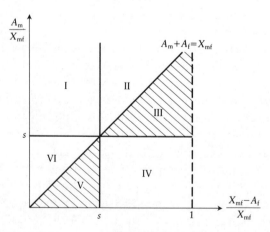

FIG. 5.3

3. *Fixed-share contract with proportional severance payments.* The output shares are fixed in advance as in the Contract 2. Additionally, in the event of separation, m must pay f the monetary equivalent[5] of some agreed fraction p $(-1 < p < 1)$ of their joint output X_{mf}. Fig. 5.4 illustrates the implications of this type of contract under the assumption that the negotiated value of p is positive, but a similar analysis can be carried out for p negative (i.e. if f is the one who has to pay). Here, m will separate if

$$A_m > (p + s)X_{mf} \qquad (5.7)$$

(areas I, II, and III), and f if

$$A_f > (1 - s)X_{mf} \qquad (5.8)$$

(areas I, V, and VI). The incidence of inefficient separation is lower than it would be under Contract 2 (area III is smaller than in Fig. 5.3), but there is now the possibility that the couple will stay together when their union is inefficient (area VII). Therefore, this type of contract is less of a disincentive to specialization than Contract 2 (and, of course, than any informal union), but it inhibits some efficient separations. Since it allows the couple to trade, by choice of p, one kind of inefficiency against another,[6] this contract type will be superior to the previous one for some probability distributions of X_{ms} and A_j, and in any case not inferior because there is always the option of choosing p equal to zero.

4. *Fixed-share contract with full severance compensation.* The couple agrees in advance that the party who gains from separation must fully compensate the other. In the event of separation, $j = m,f$ will thus receive the monetary equivalent of

$$P_j = C_j - A_j. \qquad (5.9)$$

Then, m will initiate a separation if

$$A_m > P_f + sX_{mf} \qquad (5.10)$$

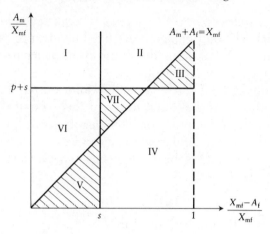

FIG. 5.4

or, in view of (5.9), if

$$A_f + A_m > X_{mf}. \tag{5.11}$$

Since the latter is also true of f, the couple will separate if and only if their union turns out to be inefficient. If both partners had the same information about their respective best alternatives, this contract type would dominate the last two because it would ensure efficient separations without creating disincentives to special-ization (the partner investing in home-specific human capital would get the return negotiated at marriage, whether or not the marriage survives). But, typically, m knows A_m better than f, and f knows A_f better than m. Therefore, each party has an incentive to understate its own best alternative, and to expend resources on trying to persuade the courts that the other side is understating his or hers. The problem does not arise in Contract 3, where levels of compensation are independent of best alternatives.

Depending on personal circumstances and transaction costs, a couple could thus find that one or other of these contracts[7] is preferable to no contract. We must investigate, next, whether a publicly regulated contract would do any better.

5.4. *The Public Contract*

A public contract of marriage—or, simply, a marriage contract as generally understood—differs from a private one in that the State is itself a party to the contractual relationship, not merely a notary recording the outcome of private negotiations. From the point of view of the State, the main justification for this intrusion is to represent the interests of the children, who cannot, of course, be parties to the contract. In economic terms, the impossibility of assigning rights to someone who does not yet exist gives rise to an externality, which in the absence of public regulation could lead to inefficiency.[8] Indeed, all the usual arguments for public regulation of marital relationships (e.g. the public interest in a stable home life as a foundation for a stable society) can be couched in terms of externalities.

Another important difference between a public and a private marriage contract is that the former does not make explicit provision for the division of the joint home-product between the spouses during the marriage period, and leaves any severance payment (alimony) to be determined, within broad parameters fixed by law, by an official arbitrator (divorce court). The absence of agreed rules for the division of X_{mf} is, as we have seen, generally undesirable because it may give rise to opportunistic bargaining after marriage. However, the expectation that in case of divorce a court would award j a (positive or negative) payment equivalent to P_j, sets a lower bound $(A_j j + P_j j)$ to the share of X_{mf} that j can be forced to accept.

The scope for post-marital bargaining under a public-contract regime could thus be small enough for the associated transaction costs to be lower than those involved in negotiating a private contract. Suppose, for example, that the official arbitrator set P_j always equal to the difference between the share of domestic output that j could have privately negotiated at the date of marriage (the 'going rate' for someone with j's characteristics) and A_j. If that were correctly anticipated by the spouses, the public contract would then work like a private contract of type 4, without the transaction costs! In reality, however, the divorce courts may not be able to gauge marriage market conditions so precisely,[9] and might be guided by considerations other than compensation in setting severance payments.

The main reason for departing from the compensation principle is, as already pointed out, the presence of children. If, in the event of divorce, the court sets the level of provision for the maintenance of children above the level that parents would have otherwise chosen, that will either reduce the incidence of divorce or, if anticipated by the marriage market, reduce the incidence of marriage. The same will be true if, in the interest of the children or for any other 'external' reason, the law imposes a cooling-off period during which the divorce is not final and the estranged partners are not allowed to remarry. The same will be true, also, if custody of the children is awarded to someone other than the parents, but the parents are still obliged to pay for the children's maintenance.

From society's point of view, the argument for State intervention in the marriage sphere is thus clear: the presence of externalities, due primarily to the impossibility of making children a party to the marriage contract, justifies public regulation. Costs of one kind or another, imposed by the State on the parents in the interest of their children and of society at large, may thus be regarded as Pigovian taxes, and any inducements to choose a public contract as Pigovian subsidies.[10]

From the couple's point of view, the argument for a public contract is not so clear-cut. If we discount the weight of tradition, it must be that the transaction costs associated with a privately negotiated contract outweigh the benefits, or that the net benefit of such a contract is outweighed by the fiscal and other inducements attaching to a public contract. Whether couples are correct in their assessment of the comparative costs and benefits of private and public marriage contracts is another matter. Evidence that women with children suffer financially from divorce[11] suggests, since private contracts are rare, that the interests of the marriage partner who specializes in home-related activities, typically the woman, might not be adequately protected by family law and public marriage contracts.[12]

Indeed, there are signs that, in some parts of Europe at least, we may be moving towards a situation where court awards will be aimed at ensuring that the income of the injured party does not fall below some conventionally set poverty line, rather than at compensating for the loss suffered with the break-up of the marriage.[13] Where the injured party is the one who specialized in home-production, this entails that the human-capital loss (the value of the market-specific human capital not accumulated because that person did not go out to work) will receive compensation only if, and to the extent that, the ability to earn of the person in question has fallen below some preset level. In the light of earlier discussion (see Chapter 2, and the first section of the present chapter) this is likely to further deter division of labour within the family, thus reducing even further the gain from marriage. The observed decline in the popularity of marriage may well have to do with this development, as well as with enhanced earning opportunities for women.

NOTES

1. The analysis in this section is inspired by Becker (1985).
2. Becker *et al.* (1977) view children as marriage-specific human capital, but that does not seem quite right because human capital cannot be separated from (is a characteristic of) the person who has accumulated it, while children obviously can. Pollak (1985), on the other hand, describes children as 'hostages' lending credibility to the

couple's mutual commitment. But that, too, is somewhat misleading because, as shown by Ermisch (1987*c*), in the event of separation children are by and large a liability rather than an asset for the parent left caring for them, typically the mother. The birth of a child thus introduces a bargaining asymmetry in the marital relationship and that, as we argue in the next paragraph, is a source of instability rather than stability. Indeed, evidence reported in Ermisch (1987*c*) suggests that early child-bearing *increases* the risk of marital break-down.

3. Market-specific human capital is portable between households, but not necessarily between employers, because some market-related skills may be firm-specific in just the same way as some home-related skills are household-specific. There is thus a parallel between the economic analysis of marital separations, and that of quits and lay-offs; see, for example, Mortensen (1978), Hashimoto and Yu (1980), Hall and Lazear (1984).

4. The diagrams in this and the following figures are adapted, like the accompanying analysis, from Hall and Lazear (1984), who in turn borrow from Hashimoto and Yu (1980).

5. The payment may take the form of an annuity or of a lump sum yielding for f the same utility as a consumption stream pX_{mf} for the rest of her life.

6. These inefficiencies do not arise from any *ex-ante* asymmetry in the position of the two parties to the contract because, it should be remembered, the couple can negotiate p to be positive (he compensates her, if he wants a divorce) or negative (she compensates him, if she wants a divorce). They arise, rather, from the fact that the sign and size of p is not made contingent on the arrival of new information. Suppose, for example, that the agreed p is positive, meaning that, at the time of signing the contract, she was thought to be the one who would suffer in the event of a separation. If, later, it turns out that she would benefit from separation (even without compensation), she will leave him. In that case, she will not receive compensation, but will not pay compensation either—even though he might suffer from the separation—because that contingency is not contemplated in the contract. This *ex-post* asymmetry, created by the contract itself, is one source of inefficiency. By contrast, it may turn out that he would benefit from a separation, but not enough to compensate her at the agreed level. In that case he would not leave her—even though, given a lower level of compensation (lower p), both could benefit. Hence the second type of inefficiency.

7. Yet another type of contract would have the party who wants to separate pay pX_{mf} ($0 < p < 1$) to the one who does not. This differs from Contract 3 in that the direction of the payment is not negotiated

at marriage, but made to depend on subsequent events (p becomes a penalty on the 'guilty' party). It is, however, inferior to Contract 3: as we can see by looking at Fig. 5.4, if the vertical line is shifted from s to $(p + s)$, area VII vanishes, but area V increases by more than the present area VII. In words, there is no chance that an inefficient union will persist, but that is more than compensated by the increased chance that an efficient union will break up.

8. See Meade (1952) and, for the relationship between rights and externalities, Coase (1980).

9. The problem is particularly difficult when it comes to valuing human capital. For example, if one of the partners gained a university degree while being maintained by the other, how is a court to value that degree in order to split it between the parties in the event of separation? For an analysis of this issue, see Borenstein and Courant (1987).

10. Pigovian taxes and subsidies are compulsory transfers designed to equate private costs to social costs, and private benefits to social benefits, in the presence of externalities; see Meade (1952).

11. See Ermisch (1987c).

12. While pointing out the hazards in privately negotiated marriage contracts, Weitzman (1981) argues that such contracts would protect women's interests better than the marriage law.

13. For example, a 1990 sentence by the highest civil court in Italy (Corte di Cassazione) overturned a lower-court sentence which imposed on a man (a doctor) a monthly payment to his former wife (a nurse) sufficient to bring her standard of living up to a level similar to that enjoyed before the divorce. The higher court ruled that the payment should merely be sufficient to guarantee the economically weaker party a 'dignified' standard of living, not the standard of living previously enjoyed as a result of a union which no longer exists.

PART II

Parents and Children

6

The Cost of Children

From this chapter onwards we assume that a stable relationship between a man and a woman has been established, and focus on a particular output of that union, children. Indeed, we assume for simplicity that child-rearing is the only home-production activity requiring time.

In the present chapter we examine the factors affecting the cost to the parents of having a child, under the assumption that parents have a common perception of how various forms of expenditure affect their children's well-being.

6.1. *Quality*

The total amount of goods that a person consumes over a lifetime is conditioned, one way or the other, by decisions taken by that person's parents. During childhood, consumption is directly under parental control. In adulthood, each person makes his or her own decisions, but those decisions and the outcomes of those decisions are conditioned by initial endowments of human and non-human capital, which are in turn the outcome, to some extent, of investments made by that person's parents: wealthier, healthier, and better educated people have a better chance in life. Even the gain from marriage, or from any other kind of co-operative domestic arrangement, is ultimately dependent, as we have seen, on the start of life that a person has had.

It is, of course, difficult (and we shall not try) to separate parental expenditures of time and commodities that produce goods for the child's immediate consumption, from expenditures that will increase his or her endowment of human capital at the start of adult life. For example, if parents pay for a child to have piano lessons at a young age, that may (or may not) give the child immediate pleasure, but it may also enhance the future adult's ability to make and enjoy music.[1] Similarly, if parents allocate time to take a child on outdoor pursuits, that may improve the child's future health as well as provide immediate gratification.

Let h denote the parents' joint home-time expended on a child. This will reflect market work lost by the mother during pregnancy, as well as time spent by both parents in caring for the child. Let b and e denote, respectively, bequests and the net flow of commodities from the parents to the child over the parents' lifetime. Included in e are all the out-of-pocket costs of pregnancy, as well as all expenditures incurred by the parents for the child's maintenance, education, and entertainment, net of any contribution that the grown-up child might make to the maintenance of his or her aged parents. Finally, let q represent the quality of life or, for short, the *quality* of a person, defined as the maximum amount of goods to which such a person can gain access by his or her own best endeavours over a lifetime, given the levels of parental benefactions received. We shall then write

$$q = v(b,e,h), \qquad (6.1)$$

where $v(\ )$ may be interpreted as the child's indirect utility function, reflecting in its parameters his or her preferences and economic environment, or as the parents' home-production function for q.

The function $v(\ )$ may be taken to be increasing in all its arguments and quasi-concave. We shall assume, in other words, that parental generosity does improve the quality of a child's life, and that a balanced mix of parental attention and commodity transfers (during the parents' lifetime or at their death) is better than too much of the one and too little of the other. As the reader will recall from Section 2.3, joint home-time is itself 'produced' by means of another quasi-concave production function which uses as factors the home-time of the two parents.

6.2. *Cost*

Let ϕ denote the rate of benefits payable to the parents for each additional child, and $(\tau - 1)$ the rate of tax on bequests, expressed in terms of the net estate.[2] Recall that the total opportunity cost of the parents' joint home-time is $W^{mf}(H_{mf}, w_m, w_f)$, as explained in Section 2.3, and that the only time-consuming domestic activities are now assumed to be those associated with the birth and care of children. Recall, further, that w_j is the wage rate of j, net of tax, and let m now stand for mother and f for father. The net cost to the parents of efficiently bringing up n children of quality q is found by minimizing $[(\tau b + e - \phi)n + W^{mf}(nh, w_m, w_f)]$, subject to (6.1). This cost,[3] denoted by Z, can be written as

$$Z = Z^{mf}(n, q, \tau, w_m, w_f, \phi) \equiv (\tau b^* + e^* - \phi)n \\ + W^{mf}(nh^*, w_m, w_f), \tag{6.2}$$

where b^*, e^*, and h^* denote the cost-minimizing levels of bequests, expenditure, and joint parental time per child.

It is clear from (6.2) that the *cost-of-children function* $Z^{mf}(\ )$ is increasing in n, q, and τ, and decreasing in ϕ. While the relationship with ϕ is obviously linear, that with τ is concave because a rise in the marginal cost of bequests would induce parents to substitute b with e and h. Since an increase in the net wage rate of either parent would raise the marginal cost of joint home-time,

$$w \equiv W_H^{mf}(nh^*, w_m, w_f), \tag{6.3}$$

it is also clear that $Z^{mf}(\ )$ is increasing and concave in w_m and w_f.

Clearly, b^* and W^{mf} cannot be negative, but e^* can, because lifetime transfers from parents to children could be smaller than transfers in the opposite direction. Therefore, it is possible for Z to be negative. Indeed, if ϕ is large enough, Z can be negative even with e^* positive. If parents are sufficiently mean, or the State sufficiently generous, towards children, having children could thus be a lucrative activity.

6.3. *The Price of Quantity and the Price of Quality*

If n or q increase a little, the total cost of children varies by

$$Z_n = \tau b^* + e^* + w h^* - \phi \qquad (6.4)$$

or

$$Z_q = \left[\tau \frac{\partial b^*}{\partial q} + \frac{\partial e^*}{\partial q} + w \frac{\partial h^*}{\partial q} \right] n, \qquad (6.5)$$

respectively. We shall refer to Z_n as the *price of quantity*, and to Z_q as the *price of quality*.[4]

We are now interested to ascertain how exogenous changes in w_m, w_f, ϕ, and τ affect the prices of child quantity and quality, because that is one way in which such changes may alter parental behaviour. Starting with child benefits, it is clear that, since ϕ reduces Z_n but does not affect Z_q, any rise in ϕ will make it relatively cheaper for parents to have more children than to improve the quality of life of those they already have. By contrast, an increase in w_m, w_f, or τ may raise both Z_n and Z_q. To establish whether their ratio rises or falls, we shall then need to be more specific about the technology of child-rearing.

Let b^0, e^0, h_m^0, and h_f^0 denote the minimum amounts of bequests, lifetime transfers, maternal time, and paternal time necessary to raise a child of whatever quality. Realistically, h_m^0 must be positive because it will include the shortest possible time for which the mother has to withdraw from the labour market during pregnancy, and in order actually to give birth, plus the shortest possible time that she will need to spend with the new-born child. By contrast, h_f^0 will be zero because the father's time is not absolutely essential. Similarly, b^0 will be zero because, on the one hand, bequests are not essential to the birth and survival of a child and, on the other, no child needs to accept an onerous benefaction (a negative b). As for e_0, that may be negative, because the maximum that a child can contribute to the maintenance of his or her parents may be larger than the minimum that parents need to spend to keep the young child alive.

Above h_m^0, however, maternal time can be substituted with paternal time in the production of h, as explained in Sections 2.3 and 5.1. Similarly, above e_0, lifetime transfers can be substituted with bequests and joint parental time in the 'production' of q. In line with the procedure followed in Chapters 2 and 3 for home-production generally, we shall also assume that the production of q is characterized by constant returns to scale, leaving it for later to introduce economies and diseconomies of scale by a different route. Let us also assume, for the time being, that neither parent is fully occupied in child-rearing, so that w is independent of n and q.

Under these assumptions, the cost of a child is given by

$$p = p_0 + p_1 q, \tag{6.6}$$

where

$$p_0 \equiv e^0 + w_m h_m^0 - \phi, \tag{6.7}$$

is the subsistence cost of the child, and p_1 is an increasing and concave function of the prices of b and h, namely τ and w. Then the total cost of children is given by

$$Z \equiv (p_0 + p_1 q)n, \tag{6.8}$$

the prices of child quantity and quality by

$$Z_n = p \tag{6.9}$$

and

$$Z_q = n p_1, \tag{6.10}$$

respectively, and the relative price of quantity to quality by

$$\frac{Z_n}{Z_q} = \frac{p_0}{np_1} + \frac{q}{n}. \tag{6.11}$$

If the rate of tax on bequests ($\tau - 1$) rises, p_1 rises with it, but p_0 stays the same. Therefore, Z_n and Z_q rise, but (Z_n/Z_q) falls. The same will be true if the father's wage rate, w_f, happens to rise. By contrast, a rise in the mother's net wage rate raises p_0 as well as p_1. Consequently, as w_m rises, Z_n and Z_q will increase, but it can be easily checked by the reader that their ratio will rise or fall according to whether the share of maternal time in the subsistence cost of a child $(w_m h_m^0/p_0)$ is larger or smaller than the elasticity of p_1 to w. Since the mother's time is the only certainly positive element in the subsistence cost of a child (and the elasticity in question is less than unity for concavity of p_1), it is then likely that (Z_n/Z_q) will rise with w_m; all the more so if ϕ is large.

In conclusion, more generous child benefits will reduce the price of quantity, but not of quality, while a harsher tax treatment of bequests will make the quantity and quality of children more expensive, but it will also make it relatively cheaper for parents to improve the quality of life of children they already have, than to have more children. Similarly, a rise in the mother's wage rate, or a cut in her marginal rate of income tax, is likely to raise the price of quantity more than that of quality. By contrast, a rise in the father's wage rate, or a cut in his marginal rate of income tax, will raise the price of quality more than that of quantity. There is, therefore, an important asymmetry between the effects of the mother's and the father's net wage rate.

6.4. *Economies and Diseconomies of Scale*

Let us now see how Z_n and Z_q are affected by changes in n and q. Given the assumptions made in the last section, a rise in q or n will have no effect on their respective prices. Under alternative assumptions, however, it is possible for Z_n or Z_q to vary with n or q. We shall say that there are economies (diseconomies) of scale in child quantity if Z_n decreases (increases) as n is raised, and that there are economies (diseconomies) of scale in child quality if Z_q decreases (increases) as q is raised.

Consider, first, the possibility of cost-sharing among children. To allow for that, we write total commodity expenditure on children as

$$E = en^\gamma, \quad 0 < \gamma \leq 1, \tag{6.12}$$

and total time expenditure on the same as

$$H = hn^\xi, \quad 0 < \xi \leq 1. \tag{6.13}$$

The reason why H might be less than nh ($\xi < 1$) is that parental time may have public-good characteristics: the appearance of a second child need not cut in half the benefit that the first child derives from each hour of parental presence. Similarly, a reason why E might be less than nc ($\gamma < 1$) is that the commodity markets may offer quantity discounts on certain items: the price per ounce of cornflakes is typically lower in larger boxes. The scope for both these forms of cost-sharing is obviously greatest if children are born in quick succession.

Another reason why γ might be less than unity is, however, that certain durable commodities (cots, perambulators, clothes) may be used sequentially by several children if their dates of birth are sufficiently far apart. It is clear, therefore, that births should be well spaced in order to make this form of cost-sharing possible, while the opposite is required to benefit from time-sharing and quantity discounts. In what follows, we take the childbearing pattern and, therefore, the values of γ and ξ as given, leaving the discussion of the choice of birth timing to Chapter 8.

Given (6.13) and (6.14), the cost of children becomes

$$Z = \tau b^* n + e^* n^\gamma - \phi n + W^{mf}(h^* n^\xi, w_m, w_f). \tag{6.14}$$

Hence,

$$Z_n = \tau b^* + \gamma e^* n^{\gamma - 1} - \phi + \xi w n^{\xi - 1} \tag{6.15}$$

and

$$Z_q = \tau \frac{\partial b^*}{\partial q} n + \frac{\partial e^*}{\partial q} n^\gamma + w \frac{\partial h^*}{\partial q} n^\xi. \tag{6.16}$$

Therefore, if there is scope for cost-sharing (i.e. at least one of γ or ξ is less than unity), there will be economies of scale in child quantity, but not in child quality.

Another possible scenario is that the mother is fully occupied in child-rearing. Since w rises, in this case, with n and h, we shall then have diseconomies of scale in both quantity and quality of children. Such diseconomies will be more pronounced if the father, also, is fully occupied at home, because w will then rise more steeply with n and h (see Section 2.3).

The picture changes somewhat if anyone of τ, w_j, or ϕ is itself dependent on n or q, in which case it will not appear as an argument of the cost-of-children function. For example, if wage rates increase with market work experience as hypothesized in Section 5.1, or part-time wage rates are lower than full-time, there could then be diseconomies in both quantity and quality, because an increase in either n or h would cause the parents a loss of earnings through a reduction in the rate of pay, as well as through a reduction in the number of hours supplied to the market (this point will be developed in Section 7.5). However, progressive income taxation would mitigate these diseconomies, because any fall in earnings would reduce the marginal rate of tax. Progressive child subsidization (ϕ increasing with n) could generate economies in child *quantity*, but not quality.

Since all these potential sources of economies or dis-economies could be present at the same time, it is, of course, possible that economies of scale would result at some levels, and diseconomies at other levels, of n or q, or that potential economies and diseconomies would approximately cancel out over the observed ranges of those variables.

6.5. *Some Estimates*

There is a substantial body of evidence on the cost of bringing up a child in a developed country. Estimates for the

USA[5] put cumulative expenditure on the average child from age zero to 18 in the $60–80,000 range at 1981 prices. These figures are similar to those available for France and Italy, but higher than those for Great Britain.[6] Estimates of time costs show a much wider range of variation, largely due to differences in the statistical methodology used to separate market hours lost through childbearing, from market hours lost for other reasons. US estimates of hours lost by the mother alone range from barely 2,000 over the mother's first fifty-five years[7] to nearly 9,300 over the child's first eighteen years[8], with a monetary value of between $20,000[9] and $50,000[10] at 1981 wage rates. The comparable figures for France are near the top of the US range in terms of hours, but nearer the bottom in terms of money, while those for Great Britain are higher in both respects.[11]

As one would expect, since they reflect parental choices, costs per child vary with parental characteristics, but there is some evidence[12] that time inputs vary much less than commodity inputs. There is, on the other hand, no information regarding economies or diseconomies of scale in child quality and no conclusive evidence of economies or diseconomies in child quantity: while some of the studies to which we have referred report commodity expenditures per child increasing with the number of children, and some report time expenditures per child decreasing as the number goes up, others show these costs to be roughly proportional to the number of children. Costs vary also with the timing of the birth. Estimates for the USA suggest that expenditure is lower the higher the parents' age at the date of birth of the child,[13] while forgone earnings are lower the higher the birth order (the second child receives less attention than the first, etc.).[14] Again in the USA, spacing (the interval between births) appears to have only a small effect on either category of cost.[15] In Great Britain, by contrast, it would seem that forgone earnings are insensitive to the date of birth of the first child, but increase with the interval between births.[16] The diversity of findings regarding scale effects and the association of scale with timing effects are obviously consistent with the theoretical considerations of the last section.

The structure of child costs makes interesting reading. Boys cost more in food, and girls in clothes, confirming the stereotype.[17] Half the cumulative market hours lost by the mother through the birth of a child is concentrated, according to US estimates, in the first five years following the birth, but it takes another five years before half the total impact on the mother's lifetime earnings is realized.[18] Both these effects are reportedly more prolonged in Great Britain.[19] This may be taken as evidence that the birth of a child reduces the mother's earnings not only directly, by reducing her labour-market participation, but also indirectly, by slowing down the growth of her marketable human capital as hypothesized in Section 5.1. Further evidence to this effect is reported in Chapter 8. As one would expect, in the light of our discussion in Section 2.4, there is also evidence that, in the USA parents have been substituting commodities for maternal time as the latter has become relatively more expensive.[20] The higher time-intensiveness of children reared in France and Great Britain, where real wage rates are on average lower than in the USA, is further evidence of the same phenomenon.

Estimates of net transfers to adult offspring are less satisfactory and more difficult to come by than those of earnings forgone and expenditures on young children. This is partly because transfers between adults typically attract tax and, therefore, tend to be either unrecorded or camouflaged. Even with full financial information, however, it would be extremely laborious to calculate the amount ultimately received by each individual from, say, age 18 onwards, in families whose members may have made, at various dates, a variety of informal, testamentary, and trust transactions in favour of a variety of beneficiaries.

What is clear, from such information as is available,[21] is that bequests are substantial. In England and Wales, for

example, the average estate (to be shared among all beneficiaries) was about £10,600 in 1974[22]—the price of a
substantial family home in those days—and there are indications that it has increased, in real terms, over the subsequent decade with the wider diffusion of home ownership.
Even that, however, was less than a fifth of the amount
actually passed on if trust property is included,[23] and still
less if gifts and unofficial transfers are taken into account.
From this we need to subtract the value of any support given
by the children to their aged parents, about which we have
no estimates. All in all, we would surmise that net transfers
(*inter vivos* or by bequest) to children from the age of 18 are
of the same order of magnitude as expenditures on children
up to 18, making a grand total per child in the $140–
210,000 range at 1981 prices. These are very imprecise
figures, but they give us a feel for the order of magnitude of
the cost of bringing up a child in a developed country.

NOTES

1. Stigler and Becker (1977) call this *beneficial addiction*.
2. The equivalent rate of tax on the *gross* estate is $[(\tau - 1)/\tau]$.
3. The reader familiar with the literature on applied demand and
   welfare analysis will have realized that the concept of cost of children
   adopted in the present chapter is different from the one of that
   literature. There, the cost of children is defined as the monetary
   equivalent of the utility directly or indirectly lost by the parents by
   having the children; see, for example, Deaton and Muellbauer
   (1986). Here, by contrast, it is defined as income actually spent or
   forgone (without any subtraction or addition of psychic gains or
   losses) in having those children.
4. This is Becker's terminology; see, for example, Becker and Lewis
   (1973).
5. Turchi (1983), Espenshade (1984).
6. Reported in Lemennicier (1988) for France, in De Santis and Righi
   (1990) for Italy, and in Joshi (1990) for Great Britain.
7. Calhoun and Espenshade (1988).
8. Turchi (1975).

9. See Lemennicier (1988) and Joshi (1990).
10. See Turchi (1975).
11. See n. 9.
12. Calhoun and Espenshade (1988).
13. Turchi (1983).
14. Calhoun and Espenshade (1988).
15. Ibid.
16. Joshi (1990).
17. Turchi (1983).
18. Calhoun and Espenshade (1988).
19. Joshi (1990).
20. Calhoun and Espenshade (1988).
21. See Blinder (1973), Harbury and Hitchens (1979).
22. Harbury and Hitchens (1979).
23. Ibid.

7

The Demand for Children

We saw in the last chapter that having a child may be costly. How costly depends on the quality of the child and on the economic environment. If the quality is sufficiently low, or the State taxes adults and subsidizes children enough, the cost of a child may even be negative, in which case parents will get more out of their children than they put in. However, the estimates reported in the last chapter suggest that the cost of the typical child, in a developed country, is positive and palpably larger than the minimum dictated by mere survival.

Now, the very fact that children are costly, no matter whether a lot or a little, and that some couples none the less have children, while they could avoid it by contraception, must mean that parents derive utility from the number or the quality of children. Additionally, the observation that some parents spend on each or some of their children more than is strictly required to bring those children into the world and keep them alive, must mean that some parents derive utility from (or feel morally compelled to take account of) the quality of the life of their children.

The present chapter seeks to explain the way in which family resources are allocated between the production of child quality and quantity (number), and that of other goods.[1]

7.1. *A Model of Family Choice*

As in the last chapter, we want to single out two particular products of domestic activities, or rather two characteristics of the same product: the quantity and the quality of children, denoted, respectively, by n and q. To this effect, we shall aggregate all the other goods into an index of parental consumption, denoted by C. As a first approximation, we shall assume that C, n, and q are determined so as to maximize

$$U = U(C,n,q), \qquad (7.1)$$

where $U(\ )$ may be interpreted as the parents' *utility function*.[2]

Implicit in this formulation are the assumptions that all decisions are taken by parents (or, at any rate, that C, n, and q are determined *as if* that were the case) and, furthermore, that children belonging to the same family have uniform quality. The first of these assumptions may be justified by saying that family plans are made before children are born —leaving open the question, to which we shall come back later, of how those plans can be realized once the children are old enough to have a say in the disposition of family resources. The second assumption has no justification other than its simplicity: we shall see in subsequent chapters that quality may turn out to be uneven, within the same family, through a combination of exogenous factors and deliberate parental choice.

That said (7.1) encompasses quite a wide range of possible situations. For a start, since q figures in the parents' utility function, it does not necessarily imply that the children's preferences do not matter—though it does imply that the children's wishes have to be interpreted and weighted by their parents. Indeed, parents could be totally selfless in their relationship with their children $(U_c \equiv 0)$[3] or, at the opposite extreme, totally selfish $(U_q \equiv 0)$. More typically, parents will not only derive utility from each of C, n, and q, but also prefer a more balanced mix of these three goods to a less balanced one. We shall assume, therefore, that the function $U(\ )$ is strictly quasi-concave.

As an alternative to saying that it represents the parents'

utility, we may interpret $U(\ )$ as the family's *welfare function* —the aggregation of the utility functions of all family members, including the children. This subtly different interpretation of the family maximand has no operational implications, since the children are not around to express their views when the family plans are made, but it does imply that parents are moved by moral considerations— moral in the strict Kantian sense. In other words, according to this interpretation, parents do what they do for their children not because they like it (an 'altruistic' parent gets more utility feeding his child than feeding himself) but because they think it is right.

Continuing to assume that child rearing is the only domestic activity requiring parental time, we can write the family budget constraint as

$$C + Z \leqslant Y_m + Y_f \equiv Y, \qquad (7.2)$$

where Z, determined by (6.2), is the cost of efficiently bringing up n children of quality q, and Y is the parents' full income. In the next three sections we shall also assume that all the assumptions underlying (6.8) apply over the relevant range, so that we may rewrite the budget constraint as

$$C + (p_0 + p_1 q)n \leqslant Y. \qquad (7.3)$$

The case where the net wage rates and, consequently, the prices of quantity and quality vary endogenously with the allocation of parental time will be examined in Section 7.5.

7.2. Exogenous Fertility

The characteristics of the solution to the family optimization problem differ according to whether the number of children born to a family is a parameter—something that just happens —or a choice variable. In the first of these two cases, parents raise the quality of each of their n children up to the point where the marginal rate of substitution of q for C is equal to the price of child quality,

$$\frac{U_q}{U_c} = Z_q \equiv n\,p_1. \tag{7.4}$$

Let us see how exogenous changes in the child-benefit rate (ϕ), in the rate of tax on bequests ($\tau - 1$), and in the father's and mother's net wage rates (w_f and w_m) affect the parents' choice of C and q.

As the benefit rate does not affect the price of quality, a rise in ϕ has no substitution effects. For any positive n, however, it will have full-income effects. The percentage changes in parental consumption and child quality attributable to a one per cent increase in the benefit rate are given by

$$\frac{\phi}{C}\frac{\partial C}{\partial \phi} = \frac{n\phi}{Y}\,\epsilon_{yc} \tag{7.5}$$

and

$$\frac{\phi}{q}\frac{\partial q}{\partial \phi} = \frac{n\phi}{Y}\,\epsilon_{yq}, \tag{7.6}$$

where ϵ_{yc} and ϵ_{yq} are the full-income elasticities of C and q (the percentage changes in C and q due to a one per cent increase in Y, holding n, p, and p_1 constant) respectively. Since it seems highly probable that parents regard their own consumption and the well-being of their children as normal goods and, therefore, that these full-income elasticities will be positive, we can then conclude that C and q will rise. Thus, an increase in the child-benefit rate will increase the well-being of children, but some of it will end up financing additional consumption for the parents.

A rise in the rate of tax on bequests will increase the price of q, thus inducing the parents to substitute C for q. Furthermore, it will have full-income effects. The percentage effects of τ on C and q are given by

$$\frac{\tau}{C}\frac{\partial C}{\partial \tau} = \frac{\tau b}{p_1 q}\left[\epsilon_{qc} - \frac{np_1}{Y}\epsilon_{yc}\right] \qquad (7.7)$$

and

$$\frac{\tau}{q}\frac{\partial q}{\partial \tau} = \frac{\tau b}{p_1 q}\left[\epsilon_{qq} - \frac{np_1}{Y}\right], \qquad (7.8)$$

where ϵ_{qc} is the compensated elasticity of C to the price of q (the percentage change in C due to a one per cent rise in np_1, holding U constant), and ϵ_{qq} is the compensated elasticity of q to its own price. Since ϵ_{qc} is positive and ϵ_{qq} is negative, it then follows that child quality will definitely fall, but parental consumption may or may not rise. C is more likely to rise in families where full income is large relative to the marginal cost of quality.

A rise in the father's net wage rate, like a rise in τ, increases the price of q because it increases the marginal cost of the parents' joint home-time (w), but, unlike τ, it increases full income. The overall effects of w_f on C and q are then

$$\frac{w_f}{C}\frac{\partial C}{\partial w_f} = \frac{w_f h_f}{p_1 q}\epsilon_{qc} + \frac{w_f L_f}{Y}\epsilon_{yc} \qquad (7.9)$$

and

$$\frac{w_f}{q}\frac{\partial q}{\partial w_f} = \frac{w_f h_f}{p_1 q}\epsilon_{qq} + \frac{w_f L_f}{Y}\epsilon_{yq}, \qquad (7.10)$$

where h_f and $L_f \equiv T - nh_f$ denote, respectively, the amount of paternal time allocated to each child and the father's labour supply. Thus, parental consumption will definitely rise, but, if the father's earnings are a large fraction of the couple's full income, the quality of children may rise too.

Similar considerations apply to the effects of a rise in the mother's net wage rate,

$$\frac{w_m}{C}\frac{\partial C}{\partial w_m} = \frac{w_m h'_m}{p_{1,}q}\epsilon_{qc} + \frac{w_m L_m}{Y}\epsilon_{yc} \qquad (7.11)$$

and

$$\frac{w_m}{q}\frac{\partial q}{\partial w_m} = \frac{w_m h'_m}{p_1 q}\epsilon_{qq} + \frac{w_m L_m}{Y}\epsilon_{yq}, \qquad (7.12)$$

where $h'_m \equiv h_m - h^0_m$ is the amount of maternal time allocated to each child over and above the essential minimum (h^0_m), and L_m is the mother's labour supply. The only qualitative difference between the effects of the father's and of the mother's net wage rate is then that child quality is more likely to be reduced by a rise in her than in his net wage rate because, by the very fact of having children, her labour supply is smaller than his.

7.3. *Endogenous Fertility*

In the case where parents are able to control the number of children, C, n, and q are chosen so as to maximize utility (or welfare), subject to the budget constraint already discussed, but subject also to the physiological constraint that they cannot have more than a certain number of children, call it n_0,

$$n \leqslant n_0. \tag{7.13}$$

If this additional constraint is binding (i.e. parents wish they could have more children than nature permits), n is held at n_0, and we are back to the case discussed in the last section. If not, parents will still equate the marginal rate of substitution of q for C to the price of quality as in (7.4), but they will also procreate up to the point where the marginal rate of substitution of n for C is equal to the price of quantity,

$$\frac{U_n}{U_c} = Z_n \equiv p. \tag{7.14}$$

Since the marginal rate of substitution of number of children for parental consumption is positive, (7.14) tells us that the cost of bringing up a child will also be positive. This is interesting because, in the case where n is pressing against its physiological ceiling, p can have any sign. Two different types of solution are thus possible. In the first, parental preferences and endowments, and the economic environment, are such that the price of n is positive and equal to the marginal rate of substitution of n for C, i.e. to the maximum that the parents are willing to pay for the desired number of children. In the second, the price is less than the marginal rate of substitution for any n up to n_0, and parents will then have as many children as they possibly can, namely n_0.

The first of these two types of solution describes the situation that prevails in developed countries, where the average child is, as we saw in the last chapter, very costly, and fertility rates are well below the physiological maximum. The second appears to be a better description of the situation that prevails in some developing countries, where fertility rates are very high and the price of a child is conversely low—maybe, in some cases, even negative, so that a child is seen by the parents as a source of income, rather than a net charge on the family.[4]

If the physiological constraint is not binding, the effects of exogenous changes in subsidy, tax, and wage rates are somewhat more complicated than in the opposite case because, first of all, a variation in any one of these variables may affect the price of quantity, as well as quality, of children. Furthermore, with three goods (C, n, and q) to choose from, it is possible that some pair of goods will be regarded by the parents as complements, rather than substitutes, over some range. For example, it is conceivable that, above a certain level of C and below a certain level of q, some parents would not contemplate increasing their own consumption without bringing about a parallel increase in the amount of family resources dedicated to the well-being of each of their children. It is also plausible that, above a certain n and below a certain q, some parents would not consider having more children without, at the same time, increasing their quality.

Let us start by examining the effects of the child-benefit rate. As we saw in the last chapter, a rise in ϕ lowers the price of child quantity, leaving the price of quality constant. As n is now a variable, this will have substitution effects in addition to the full-income effects that we encountered in the fixed-n case. The overall effects on parental consumption, number and quality of children are then given by

$$\frac{\phi}{C}\frac{\partial C}{\partial \phi} = -\frac{\phi n}{p}\left[\epsilon_{nc} - \frac{p}{Y}\epsilon_{yc}\right], \qquad (7.15)$$

$$\frac{\phi}{n}\frac{\partial n}{\partial \phi} = -\frac{\phi n}{p}\left[\epsilon_{nn} - \frac{p}{Y}\epsilon_{yn}\right], \qquad (7.16)$$

and

$$\frac{\phi}{q}\frac{\partial q}{\partial \phi} = -\frac{\phi n}{n}\left[\epsilon_{nq} - \frac{p}{Y}\epsilon_{yq}\right], \qquad (7.17)$$

where ϵ_{nc}, ϵ_{nn} and ϵ_{nq} are the compensated elasticities of, respectively, C, n, and q to the price of n, and ϵ_{yn} is the full-income elasticity of n.

Since ϵ_{nn} is negative, and assuming that parents regard the number of children as a normal good, it is clear from (7.16) that a rise in the benefit rate will induce parents to have more children. If the number of children is a substitute for both parental consumption and the quality of children, so that both ϵ_{nc} and ϵ_{nq} are positive, the overall effects of ϕ on C and q will be generally ambiguous (negative for families with sufficiently large full income). A rise in ϕ will definitely raise C if C and n are complements (ϵ_{nc} negative) or q if n and q are complements (ϵ_{nq} negative). The ratio of quality to quantity is in any case likely to fall, and will definitely fall if parental preferences are homothetic (i.e. if the indifference curves are parallel along any ray from the origin), because the relative price of quality to quantity rises with ϕ.

Next, we look at the consequences of a rise in the rate of tax on bequests ($\tau - 1$). As we saw in the last chapter, the prices of both quantity and quality will rise—the latter more than the former. The overall effects of τ on C, n, and q are thus sums of two substitution effects (one via the price of n, the other via that of q) and of a full-income effect:

$$\frac{\tau}{C}\frac{\partial C}{\partial \tau} = \frac{\tau b}{p_1 q}\left[\frac{p_1 q}{p}\epsilon_{nc} + \epsilon_{qc} - \frac{np_1}{Y}\epsilon_{yc}\right], \qquad (7.18)$$

$$\frac{\tau}{n}\frac{\partial n}{\partial \tau} = \frac{\tau b}{p_1 q}\left[\frac{p_1 q}{p}\epsilon_{nn} + \epsilon_{qn} - \frac{np_1}{Y}\epsilon_{yn}\right], \quad (7.19)$$

and

$$\frac{\tau}{q}\frac{\partial q}{\partial \tau} = \frac{\tau b}{p_1 q}\left[\frac{p_1 q}{p}\epsilon_{nq} + \epsilon_{qq} - \frac{np_1}{Y}\epsilon_{yq}\right]. \quad (7.20)$$

As a consequence, parental consumption, and the quantity and quality of children, could either rise or fall as τ rises. Contrary to what we found in the fixed-*n* case, a rise in the rate of tax on bequests could thus raise the quality of children and, if that were the case, it would paradoxically raise quality more in families which make larger bequests to each of their children! If, however, quality and quantity are complements, both will definitely fall as τ rises. In any case, quality is likely to fall (and, given homotheticity, it will) relative to quantity, because the relative price of quality to quantity rises with τ.

A rise in the father's net wage rate raises the prices of quantity and quality, and the relative price of quality to quantity. The signs of its overall effects on parental consumption, and on quantity and quality of children,

$$\frac{w_f}{C}\frac{\partial C}{\partial w_f} = \frac{w_f h_f}{p}\epsilon_{nc} + \frac{w_f h_f}{p_1 q}\epsilon_{qc} + \frac{w_f L_f}{Y}\epsilon_{yc}, \quad (7.21)$$

$$\frac{w_f}{n}\frac{\partial n}{\partial w_f} = \frac{w_f h_f}{p}\epsilon_{nn} + \frac{w_f h_f}{p_1 q}\epsilon_{qn} + \frac{w_f L_f}{Y}\epsilon_{yn}, \quad (7.22)$$

and

$$\frac{w_f}{q}\frac{\partial q}{\partial w_f} = \frac{w_f h_f}{p}\epsilon_{nq} + \frac{w_f h_f}{p_1 q}\epsilon_{qq} + \frac{w_f L_f}{Y}\epsilon_{yq}, \quad (7.23)$$

are again ambiguous in general. However, since the father's earnings are likely to account for a large share of the couple's full income, and the value of his time is likely to be only a small part of the cost of each child, the full-income effects of w_f will tend to predominate, as in the fixed-*n* case, and the overall effects on C, *n*, and *q* are again likely to be positive. The overall effect on parental consumption will definitely be positive, and the likelihood of positive overall effects on the quantity and quality of children will be reinforced, if q is a substitute for both C and n. Once again, the ratio of quality to quantity is likely to fall because the relative price rises with w_f.

Finally, a rise in the mother's net wage rate will raise the prices of quantity and quality but, as we saw in the last chapter, the relative price of quality to quantity is likely to fall (instead of rising as for a rise in the father's net wage rate). Furthermore, the full-income effects of the mother's net wage rate are unlikely to dominate the substitution effects, because the value of her time is a substantial part of the cost of a child, and her earnings are unlikely to account for a very large part of the couple's full income. Therefore, the overall effect on parental consumption,

$$\frac{w_m}{C}\frac{\partial C}{\partial w_m} = \frac{w_m h_m}{p}\,\epsilon_{nc} + \frac{w_m h'_m}{p_1\, q}\,\epsilon_{qc} + \frac{w_m L_m}{Y}\epsilon_{yc}, \quad (7.24)$$

will be positive if q is a substitute for C, but will have an ambiguous sign otherwise. By contrast, the overall effects on quantity and quality of children,

$$\frac{w_m}{n}\frac{\partial n}{\partial w_m} = \frac{w_m h_m}{p}\,\epsilon_{nn} + \frac{w_m h'_m}{p_1\, q}\,\epsilon_{qn} + \frac{w_m L_m}{Y}\epsilon_{yn} \quad (7.25)$$

and

$$\frac{w_m}{q}\frac{\partial q}{\partial w_m} = \frac{w_m h_m}{p}\,\epsilon_{nq} + \frac{w_m h'_m}{p_1\, q}\,\epsilon_{qq} + \frac{w_m L_m}{Y}\epsilon_{yq}, \quad (7.26)$$

are likely to be negative if q is a complement for n, but ambiguous otherwise. In contrast with the situation when w_f or any of the other exogenous variables rises, quality is likely to rise relative to quantity, as w_m rises, because of the likely fall in the relative price.

In conclusion, the ready availability of fertility controls, combined with conditions, typical of developed countries, that favour a generous treatment of children by their parents, makes a considerable difference to the responses of C and q to changes in the exogenous variables. In particular, child benefits cease to be a reliable policy instrument for improving the well-being of children and become, essentially, an incentive to procreation. By contrast, an increase in married women's wage rates, or a more lenient fiscal treatment of their earnings, could reduce the number of children and improve the quality of their lives.

7.4. *Fertility and Labour Supply*

Exogenous variations in wage, tax, and subsidy rates will affect not only the quality and quantity of children—in the way we have just seen—but also the amounts of bequests, lifetime expenditures, and parental time used to produce those goods. These derived effects are, however, very difficult to sign.

As in the ordinary theory of production, a change in the price of an input affects the derived demand for that input in two ways: directly, by inducing a substitution away from the input that has become relatively more expensive and, indirectly, through the effect it has on the demand for the output. The parallel is not, however, with the theory of the profit-maximizing firm, but with that of the firm (e.g. a public utility) which maximizes output subject to a budget constraint—with the additional complications, in our case, of primary endowments that can be either used in the internal production process or sold to the market, and of two tiers of intermediate products. The primary resources, here, are commodities, and the father's and mother's time. The first-tier intermediate product is joint home-time. The second-tier intermediate products are children (with a quantity and a quality dimension) and parental consumption. The final product is utility.

Suppose, for example, that the mother's wage rate rises, or that the marginal rate of tax on her earnings is reduced. As w_m rises, paternal time will be substituted for maternal time in the production of joint home-time, commodities will be substituted for joint home-time in the production of children, and child quality will be substituted for child quantity in the production of utility. Additionally, the relaxation of the budget constraint consequent upon the wage rise will result in an increased production of utility. Depending on the relative sizes of these effects, the home-time of either or both parents, and either or both forms of expenditure on children, could increase or decrease.

The reason why, in Chapter 2, we were able to be fairly definite about the effects of w_f and w_m on H_f and H_m is, of course, that the model used there (with parental consumption and children aggregated into one good) is a simplified version of the present one. Since, it will be remembered, the predictions of the simplified model about the effects of w_f and w_m on H_f and H_m are supported by the empirical evidence, it will be interesting to combine those predictions with those of the present model about the effects of the same variables on n and q. Recalling that both n and H_m are likely to decrease if w_m rises, and to increase if w_f rises, we can then conclude that n and H_m are likely to move in the same direction if wage rates change one at the time. Depending on their elasticities to w_m and w_f, however, n and H_m *could* move in opposite directions if wage rates move together. The empirical observation that fertility and female labour-market participation move generally in opposite directions,[5] but together on occasions, can thus be explained in terms of wage elasticities of maternal home-time and quantity of children, and of growth rates of male and female wage rates.

7.5. *Fertility and Human Capital*

The analysis of the last three sections was based on the assumption that ϕ, τ, w_m, and w_f are independent of family choices and, furthermore, that Z_n and Z_q are independent of, respectively, the quantity and quality of children. As we saw in the last chapter, however, this is not necessarily the case—for a variety of possible reasons. Rather than attack the problem in its full generality, which is extremely complicated and does not yield interpretable results, we shall now explore a particular deviation from the assumptions made in the preceding sections. We shall assume, as in (5.1), that wage rates are proportional to the stock of market-specific human capital of the recipient, and that human capital increases with market experience as in (5.2).

As even this seemingly innocuous extension of the model increases its complexity very considerably, we shall have to simplify it in other respects. We shall assume, first of all, that

$$U = U(C,B), \qquad (7.27)$$

where $U(\ )$ is quasi-concave, and

$$B \equiv nq \qquad (7.28)$$

may be interpreted as a quality-adjusted index of fertility. This formulation rules out the possibility that, with n variable, q could be a complement for C or n. Another simplification will be to assume that, above the vital minimum h_m^0, maternal time is perfectly substitutable with the time of the father or of hired helpers in the upbringing of a child. Assuming, further, that the wage rates payable to hired helpers are always lower than those that the parents themselves could earn, h_m^0 is all the parental time that a child will get. Yet another simplification, along similar lines, will be to assume that, above e^0, lifetime expenditure on children is perfectly substitutable with bequests. We can then write

$$q = v(I), \qquad (7.29)$$

where

$$I \equiv \tau b + e - e^0 \qquad (7.30)$$

is the total investment per child in excess of the minimum, and $v(\ )$ is strictly concave.

Setting h_m^0 equal to unity, by measuring time in terms of number of children, the mother's labour supply will now be given by

$$L_m = T - n, \qquad (7.31)$$

and her stock of marketable human capital by

$$k_m = k_m^0 + \beta_m L_m, \quad \beta_m > 0, \qquad (7.32)$$

where k_m^0 is the initial endowment (a measure of her innate talent and of her education, as well as of her work experience before marriage) and β_m the rate at which that capital increases with work experience. Her wage rate is endogenously determined by

$$w_m = \omega_m k_m, \qquad (7.33)$$

where ω_m is the market rate of return to k_m. The father's labour supply, by contrast, will be simply T. His wage rate, given by

$$w_f = \omega_f (k_f^0 + \beta_f T), \quad \beta_f > 0, \qquad (7.34)$$

and his earnings will thus be independent of n.

Under these assumptions, the budget constraint may be written as

$$C + (e^0 + I - \phi)n \leqslant A + w_m L_m \equiv Y, \qquad (7.35)$$

where A is defined as the sum of property income and paternal earnings. Note that Y now stands for actual and not full income, because it does not include the potential earnings forgone by the mother for having children. To maximize (7.27) subject to (7.13) and (7.35), the parents will equate the marginal utility of income spent on themselves to that of income spent on each child,

$$U_C = U_B v'(I). \qquad (7.36)$$

If the physiological constraint (7.13) is not binding, they will also equate the marginal rate of substitution of quantity for quality to the price of quantity,

$$\frac{v(I)}{v'(I)} = p_0 + I + \beta_m \omega_m L_m \equiv p. \qquad (7.37)$$

Notice that the cost of an extra child, p, now includes the potential wage rises missed by the mother for having that child ($\beta \omega L_m$), as well as expenses actually incurred

$(e^0 + I - \phi)$ and wage actually forgone (w_m). We can think of the first of these three elements of cost as of a capital gain forgone: the appreciation in the woman's stock of human capital that will not be realized if she stays at home for a unit of time.

If the physiological constraint (7.13) is not binding, a rise in ϕ will clearly raise n,

$$\frac{\phi}{n} \frac{\partial n}{\partial \phi} = -\frac{\phi}{p} \epsilon_{nn} + \frac{n\phi}{Y} \epsilon_{yn}, \qquad (7.38)$$

but its effect on I and, therefore, on q will be ambiguous

$$\frac{\phi}{I} \frac{\partial I}{\partial \phi} = -\frac{\phi}{p} \epsilon_{ni} + \frac{n\phi}{Y} \epsilon_{yi}. \qquad (7.39)$$

We can be sure that I and q will rise with ϕ only if (7.13) is binding. On the other hand, a rise in k_f^0, β_f or ω_f will raise w_f and A. Since this has only income effects on the choice variables, the quantity and quality of children will then rise with the father's wage rate, while his labour supply will stay constant and the mother's will fall. Unless, of course, n is held at its physiological ceiling, in which case all that happens is a rise in quality. These predictions are in line with those of the last three sections.

The role of k_m^0, β_m and ω_m is slightly more problematic. Their effects on I (and q),

$$\frac{k_m^0}{I} \frac{\partial I}{\partial k_m^0} = \frac{\omega_m k_m^0}{p} \epsilon_{ni} + \frac{\omega_m k_m^0 L_m}{Y} \epsilon_{yi}, \qquad (7.40)$$

$$\frac{\beta_m}{I} \frac{\partial I}{\partial \beta_m} = \frac{\beta_m \omega_m L_m}{p} \left[2\,\epsilon_{ni} + \frac{pL_m}{Y} \right], \qquad (7.41)$$

and

$$\frac{\omega_m}{I} \frac{\partial I}{\partial \omega_m} = \frac{\omega_m (k_m + \beta_m L_m)}{p} \epsilon_{ni} + \frac{w_m L_m}{Y} \epsilon_{yi} \qquad (7.42)$$

are clearly positive, but those on n (and L_m)

$$\frac{k_m^0}{n} \frac{\partial n}{\partial k_m^0} = \frac{\omega_m k_m^0}{p} \epsilon_{nn} + \frac{\omega_m k_m^0 L_m}{Y} \epsilon_{yn}, \qquad (7.43)$$

$$\frac{\beta_m}{n}\frac{\partial n}{\partial \beta_m} = \frac{\beta_m \omega_m L_m}{p}\left[2\,\epsilon_{nn} + \frac{pL_m}{Y}\epsilon_{yn} \right], \quad (7.44)$$

$$\frac{w_m}{n}\frac{\partial n}{\partial \omega_m} = \frac{w_m + \beta_m \omega_m L_m}{p}\epsilon_{nn} + \frac{w_m L_m}{Y}\epsilon_{yn}, \quad (7.45)$$

have an ambiguous sign. Also ambiguous, in view of (7.32) and (7.33), are their effects on w_m. None the less, the number of children born to a woman is still likely to move in the opposite direction from her wage rate and labour supply—just as in the model with exogenously given wage rates, and for the same reason, namely that the mother's time has relatively greater weight in the cost of a child than in the family income. Indeed, that argument gains strength here that wage rates and number of children are simultaneously determined, because the father is fully specialized in income-raising activities.

7.6. *Some Empirical Evidence*

The evidence on the relationship between birth and wage rates is unequivocal. Econometric estimates for the USA put the elasticity of fertility to the average female wage rate at -1.73, and the elasticity of the same to the average male wage rate at $+1.31$.[6] Estimates of the same elasticity for Europe,[7] put it at -1.34 with regard to female wage rates and $+1.26$ with regard to male wage rates, if calculated on the basis of average wage and fertility levels typical of the more prosperous regions, but -0.76 for female and $+1.03$ for male wage rates when calculated for the less prosperous regions. These estimates imply that a 10 per cent rise in female wages would *lower* the birth rate by between about 8 and 17 per cent, according to the level of prosperity of the region, while a similar rise in the male wage rate would *raise* the birth rate by between 10 and 13 per cent. A simultaneous 10 per cent rise in male and female wage rates would lower the birth rate by up to 4 per cent (but, in less prosperous areas, could raise it slightly).

All this goes a long way towards explaining why birth rates have fallen so dramatically in all industrialized countries since the post-war period,[8] in concomitance with a steady rise in wage rates generally, and with a gradual narrowing down of the gap between male and female wage rates. It explains, furthermore, why fertility tends to be lower in low unemployment areas, where strong demand for labour tends to equalize male and female wage rates at a high level, than in high unemployment areas, where wage rates are low, and female labour more easily exploited.[9]

Together with the evidence of the high cost of children in industrialized countries, reported in Chapter 6, these estimates verify the theoretical prediction made in the present chapter that fertility will be low (by parental choice, not for any physiological reason) in societies and strata of society where the cost of children is (again by parental choice) high.[10] They are also consistent with the theoretical prediction that, irrespective of whether or not wage rates depend on work experience, a rise in the mother's wage rate is likely to be associated with lower fertility, while a rise in the father's is likely to be associated with higher fertility.

The implications for fertility and female labour-market participation of different tax treatments of married women's earnings, and of different child-benefit regimes, are well illustrated by a comparative study of Sweden and West Germany.[11] In Sweden, where husband and wife are taxed separately, and child benefits (in money and in kind) are generous, particularly for the working mother, both fertility *and* female labour-market participation[12] are considerably higher than in West Germany, where couples are jointly taxed and benefits less generous. The higher fertility of Sweden is consistent with the theoretical prediction that the effect of child benefits on the demand for quantity of children is unequivocally positive, while the effect of the mother's after-tax wage rate has an ambiguous sign. The higher female labour-market participation can be explained partly by the fact that a higher after-tax maternal wage rate induces a substitution of commodities and paternal time for maternal time in the raising of children, and partly by the fact that the Swedish public sector provides free or low-cost substitutes for the mother's home-time (crèches, etc.).

Finally, our assumption that bequests are the result of deliberate choice, rather than wealth accidentally left over after paying for the donor's retirement, is consistent with evidence[13] that the size of the estate *increases* with the age of death of the donor.

NOTES

1. This chapter draws on Becker (1960, 1981) and Willis (1973). The particular model used and results obtained are those of Cigno (1986) and, for Sec. 7.5, of Cigno (1988*b*).
2. This is the standard formulation of the family maximand; cf. Becker (1960, 1981), Willis (1973). The less general form $U(C, nq)$ is used by some authors to rule out complementarity.
3. Subject to some lower bound on C, to ensure their own survival.
4. As Caldwell (1978) puts it, 'two types of societies can be distinguished: one of stable high fertility, where there should be no economic gain accruing to the family (or to those dominant within it) from lower fertility levels, and the other in which economic rationality alone would dictate zero reproduction.'
5. Blundell and Walker (1982) and Colombino and De Stavola (1985), among many others, report evidence of negative correlation between fertility and female labour supply.
6. Butz and Ward (1979). Similar findings are reported by Ermisch (1979) for the UK.
7. See Winegarden (1984).
8. In Italy, for example, total fertility (the average number of live births per woman) fell from 2.6 in 1965 to 1.3 in 1988. Similar trends are reported for the other major West European countries (from 2.8 to 1.8 in France and in the UK, from 2.5 to 1.4 in West Germany) and for the industrialized world as a whole. See Monnier (1989).
9. In 1980, for example, total fertility was still above replacement level (the level required to keep the population constant) in high-

unemployment, low-wage European countries (3.2 in Ireland, 2.2 in Greece, Portugal, and Spain), but well below it in low-unemployment, high-wage ones (1.4 in West Germany, 1.5 in Denmark and Switzerland, 1.6 in Austria, the Netherlands, and Belgium, 1.7 in Italy and Sweden); cf. Monnier (1989). Further support for the hypothesis under discussion comes from the observation that the low total fertility of Italy (1.7) was the average of a much lower total fertility rate (1.3) in the heavily industrialized, effectively zero-unemployment north, of a moderately lower rate (1.5) in the prosperous, high-employment centre, and of an above-replacement rate (2.2) in the high-unemployment south.

10. Further corroborating evidence comes from an economic study of US data, Behrman *et al.* (1982), which rejects the hypothesis that children might be regarded by their parents as a profitable investment.

11. See Gustafsson (1985).

12. Over the 1975–80 period, total fertility per woman ranged between 1.76 and 1.68 in Sweden, compared with 1.45 to 1.38 in West Germany. Over the same period, the female labour force was 67.6–74.1 per cent of the relevant age group in Sweden, compared with 49.6–50 in West Germany.

13. See, among others, Mirer (1980).

8

The Timing of Births

The last two chapters were concerned with the study of *completed fertility* (the total number of children born to a woman over her lifetime). In the present chapter we look at factors determining the *tempo of fertility* (the distribution of births over the mother's lifetime).

The introduction of timing considerations complicates the analysis considerably, because it becomes necessary to account for substitutions and interactions among fertility, expenditure, and earnings at different dates. An explicitly dynamic model is, therefore, necessary. Furthermore, the nature of the problem in hand makes accounting for the effects of uncertainty unavoidable.

As we shall see in the final section, the introduction of timing considerations in the family decision process helps to explain the sharp fluctuations in *period fertility* (the number of children born in a particular country or region over a particular period, usually the year) that have characterized the developed part of the world since the end of the Second World War.

8.1. *A Dynamic Model of Family Choice*

We have already reported, in Section 6.5, on empirical evidence that the birth of a child reduces the mother's earnings not only directly, by reducing her labour-market participation, but also indirectly, by slowing down the growth of her marketable human capital. There is also evidence that, while the first of these effects is mainly concentrated in the early years of the child's life, the second lingers on much longer.[1] It does seem, therefore, that a dynamic version of the human-capital model examined in Section 7.5 could capture the essential elements of the parental decision to anticipate or postpone the birth of a child.[2]

Parents-to-be will then be assumed to maximize a utility function that, as in (7.31), has for argument B and C, where B is a quality-adjusted index of completed fertility, and C an index of parental consumption. However, we shall now make the values of these indices dependent on the time of occurrence of births and expenditures by redefining the fertility index as

$$B = \sum_{t=M}^{D} v_t(I_t)B_t \qquad (8.1)$$

and the consumption index as

$$C = \sum_{t=M}^{D} u_t(C_t), \qquad (8.2)$$

where B_t denotes the rate of birth at t, I_t the amount invested in a child born at t (the present value at t of all expenditures, including the cost of any bequests, incurred by the parents on behalf of that child over and above the necessary minimum, e^0, which includes the cost of procuring the birth of a child) and C_t the amount spent for the parents' own consumption at t. D and M denote, respectively, the date of death (assumed, for simplicity, to be the same for both partners) and the date of marriage (meaning by that the date of formation of the union, whether or not it was legalized) of the parents.

The function $u_t(\ )$, assumed increasing and strictly concave, may be interpreted as the 'specific utility' to the parents of consuming at t. Its dependence on t allows for the possibility that parents might be impatient to consume (i.e. that they might discount the utility of future consumption). The function $v_t(\ )$, also increasing and strictly concave, may be similarly interpreted as the 'specific utility' to the parents of the quality of life of a child born at t. Time-dependence, in this case, may reflect impatience to have children or, more generally, dependence of the joy of parenthood on the age or length of marriage of the parents. It will also reflect an awareness on the part of the parents that the probability of having a child decreases, for any given I_t, as the mother approaches the end of her fecund life-span, at date t^*, and is zero after that.

As in Section 7.5, we set the minimum amount of maternal time required by each child equal to unity, so we can write the wife's labour supply at t as

$$L_t = m - B_t, \tag{8.3}$$

where m is her work capacity. Her (net) wage rate at t is then given by

$$w_t = \omega k_t, \tag{8.4}$$

where

$$k_t = k_M + \beta \sum_{\tau = M}^{t-1} L_\tau \tag{8.5}$$

is her stock of market-specific human capital at t, and ω the market rate of return (net of the marginal rate of tax on her earnings) to that capital.

Assuming that the couple can borrow or lend at the interest rate $(r - 1)$, their lifetime budget constraint is

$$\sum_{t = M}^{D} [C_t + (I_t + e^0 - \phi)B_t]r^{M-t} \leq A + \sum_{t = M}^{D} L_t w_t r^{M-t}, \tag{8.6}$$

where A now stands for the sum of the couple's assets at the date of marriage, plus the present value, at that same date, of the husband's (net) lifetime earnings. As before, ϕ is the rate of child benefits. The couple will then choose a sequence $\{B_t, C_t, I_t\}$ that maximizes (7.31), subject to (8.6) and to the physiological restrictions

$$0 \leq B_t \leq \bar{B}_t, \tag{8.7}$$

where $\bar{B}_t$ (assumed no greater than m for any t, and equal to zero for $t > t^*$) is the maximum possible level of B_t, for each t[3].

If (8.7) is not binding[4] for any t, the chosen sequence will satisfy the conditions

$$\frac{u'_t\,(C_t)}{u'_{t+1}(C_{t+1})} = r, \qquad (8.8)$$

$$\frac{v'_t\,(I_t)}{v'_{t+1}(I_{t+1})} = r, \qquad (8.9)$$

and

$$\frac{[p_{t+1}/v_{t+1}(I_{t+1})]}{[p_t/v_t(I_t)]} = r, \qquad (8.10)$$

where

$$p_t = e^0 - \phi + I_t + w_t + \beta\omega \sum_{\tau=t+1}^{D} L_\tau r^{t-\tau} \qquad (8.11)$$

is the full cost of having a child (the price of child quantity) at t. As in (7.41), that cost is thus the sum of an actual outlay $(e^0 - \phi + I_t)$, an income forgone (w_t), and a human capital gain forgone (dependent on future employment).

Conditions (8.8) and (8.9) are easily recognizable as instances of the general principle (the Ramsey–Keynes rule) that any form of expenditure must be distributed over time so that its marginal utility will decline at the rate of interest. By contrast, (8.10) is an *intertemporal arbitrage* condition: the cost of having a child at date t must be equal, after quality normalization, to the cost of having a child at date $(t + 1)$ discounted back to date t at the interest factor r. If $[(p_{t+1}/v_{t+1})/r]$ were less than (p_t/v_t), it would in fact pay the couple to delay until $(t + 1)$ any birth planned for t, and to lend the sum thus saved at the interest rate $(r - 1)$. Conversely, if $[(p_{t+1}/v_{t+1})/r]$ were more than (p_t/v_t), the couple would borrow, at t, the sum required to anticipate any birth planned for date $(t + 1)$. Therefore, along any optimal fertility profile, the price of child quantity (normalized for quality) will grow at the rate of interest.

What can we deduce from these conditions about the time profile of birth rate, expenditure per child, and parental consumption? Without additional assumptions,[5] it seems, not very much. If $u_t(\ )$ is iso-elastic, parental consumption will increase or decrease with the passage of time according to whether the rate at which parents discount the utility of future consumption is lower or higher than the rate of interest. Similarly, if $v_t(\ )$ is iso-elastic, we shall find that whether the amount spent on a child is higher or lower at higher birth parities depends on whether the rate at which the quality is perceived to decline (for any given level of expenditure) as the mother gets older is lower or higher than the rate of interest. In general, therefore, parents will not treat all their children equally. They may treat the first-born better than the second, the second-born better than the third and so on—or the other way round. If the perceived rate of decline of child quality is not constant, we may even find, as folklore has it, that the middle child comes off worst.

If $v_t(\ )$ is iso-elastic, we shall also have that p_t grows at the same proportional rate as I_t. Therefore, since $(e^0 - \phi)$ is a constant, the opportunity-cost component (income plus capital gain forgone) of p_t also will grow at the same proportional rate as I_t. If the perceived rate of quality decline were higher than the rate of interest, the opportunity cost of a child would then decrease with the passage of time and become lower for each successive birth. Let that be the case.[6] What does that tell us about the behaviour of birth rates?

It is clear from (8.11) that postponing the birth of a child raises the income loss and lowers the capital loss associated with that birth. For example, if r were equal to unity, delaying a birth from date t to date $(t + 1)$ would increase the income forgone by $\beta\omega(m - B_t)$, and reduce the capital gain forgone by $\beta\omega(m - B_{t+1})$. Therefore, with a zero rate of interest, a declining opportunity cost would imply a declining birth rate. Since the rate of interest is normally positive, however, the capital-loss element of the cost of a

child will fall, as the birth is postponed, by less than
$\beta\omega(m - B_{t+1})$, and precisely by that amount minus the
interests on the human-capital gain forgone by having a
child at t. As the capital loss at t is lower, the higher the birth
rate at $(t + 1)$, a declining opportunity cost may thus imply a
fluctuating birth profile. In other words, parents may find it
optimal to have their children in batches, rather than spaced
out over the fecund period.[7]

8.2. *Effects of Personal Characteristics and the Economic Environment*

We are now interested to find out how birth profiles differ
for couples with different characteristics, and for different
economic environments. Given the complexity of the dynamic
interactions, however, it seems that that cannot be done at
the present level of generality.[8] What follows is, therefore,
no more than the analysis of a special case.

Consider the following parameterization:

$$u_t(C_t) \equiv C_t^\gamma \, g^{(M-t)} \qquad 0 < \gamma < 1 \qquad (8.12)$$

and

$$v_t(I_t) \equiv I_t^\alpha \, a^{-t}, \qquad 0 < \alpha < 1 \qquad (8.13)$$

where t is now measured from the beginning of the woman's
fecund life-span (supposed to have occurred before the date
of marriage), and the interval between any two dates is
taken to be a year. We may interpret the constant $(g - 1)$ as
the rate of discount on the utility of parental consumption.
Similarly, we may interpret $(a - 1)$ as the rate of discount on
the utility of having children. Realistically, this last rate of
discount must be large enough for v_t to be virtually zero
(whatever the value of I_t) and, therefore, for B_t and I_t to be
chosen close to zero from around $t = 40$ onwards. Therefore, $(a - 1)$ must be at least 10 per cent $(a \geqslant 1.1)$.[9]

Given (8.8)–(8.13), the time profiles of C_t, I_t and B_t are
given by[10]

$$C_t = C_M(r/g)^{[(t-M)/(1-\gamma)]}, \tag{8.14}$$

$$I_t = I_M(r/a)^{[(t-M)/(1-\alpha)]}, \tag{8.15}$$

and

$$B_t = m + iI_M(r/a)^{(t-M)} - (m + iI_M - B_M)\frac{\sin tx}{\sin Mx}r^{[(t-M)/2]}, \tag{8.16}$$

where x is an angle with cosine equal to $r^{-1/2}$ and

$$i = i(\beta,\omega,r) \tag{8.17}$$

is positive and decreasing in all its arguments for $r \geqslant 1.1$. B_M and C_M respectively denote births and parental consumption over the first year of marriage, while I_M is the amount invested on any child born in that year.

It is clear from (8.14) that parental consumption may either grow or decline steadily over married life. By contrast, we can see from (8.15) that I_t will decline steadily over married life for realistic values of r and a, because the (real) rate of interest is not likely to be higher than 10 per cent, while the rate of discount on the utility of children cannot be less than 10 per cent. Therefore, the first-born child will get more than the second, etc.

For its part (8.16) tells us that, again for realistic values of r and a, the birth rate has a downward trend (described by the first two terms on the right of the equality sign). It also tells us that the birth rate will fluctuate around the trend whenever the interest rate is positive ($r > 1$), and that these fluctuations (described by the third right-hand-side term) will tend to die down with the passage of time. Therefore, if borrowing is costly as it normally is, it is optimal for parents to have children in batches. That, it will be recalled, is a possibility in the general model also. For particular ranges of values of the parameters, however, (8.16) displays just one significant fluctuation—meaning that it is optimal to have all children close together, in one batch. For other parameter ranges, by contrast, fluctuations are many but very small, so that the birth rate declines more or less in geometric progression—meaning that it is optimal to space births out over married life, at longer and longer intervals.

Given (8.14)–(8.16), or similar equations in the case of different parameterizations, the choice of the sequence $\{B_t, C_t, I_t\}$ reduces to the choice of the values of B_t, C_t, and I_t in the first year after marriage. The consequences of changes of economic environment, or of differences in personal characteristics, on the number and time-distribution of births are thus the sum of two effects: a direct effect on the shape of the optimal time profile, and an indirect effect through the choice of B_M and I_M. The latter affect the fertility profile because, as is clear from (8.16), a rise in B_M raises completed fertility (lifts the trend line up), while a rise in I_M raises the tempo (tilts the trend line forward). Furthermore, a rise in B_M makes fluctuations smaller.

The effects of environmental changes and personal differences on the choice of B_M, C_M, and I_M are rather complicated and generally ambiguous. However, it can be shown[11] that, if income effects are dominated by substitution effects and the marginal utility of B does not fall (i.e. parenthood does not lose its charm) 'too quickly' as B is increased, then A has a positive effect on B_M and I_M, while K_M and e^0 have negative effect on B_M and positive effect on I_M. Since A, K_M, e^0, and ϕ do not figure in (8.16), none of them has a direct effect on the fertility profile. We can then conclude that, under the stated assumptions, couples with larger assets or larger paternal earnings (higher A) will have more children[12] and sooner in married life. Furthermore, couples will be less inclined to cluster births together (fertility fluctuations will be smaller). By the same reasoning, women who enter marriage better endowed with market-specific human capital (higher K_M) will have fewer children and sooner, and will also tend to cluster births more. A rise in the set-up cost of a child, e^0, will induce parents to have fewer children but sooner, and to cluster births more, while more generous child benefits (higher ϕ) will do the exact opposite.

By contrast β, ω, and r have direct effects on the fertility profile, but their indirect effects cannot be signed under any plausible set of assumptions. Their direct effect, since i is decreasing in all of them, is to tilt the fertility profile backwards. If the indirect effects are small in comparison with the direct ones, a generalized rise in the net wage rates of married women (higher ω), or a rise in the rate of interest (higher r), will then lower the tempo of fertility. An interest rate rise will also induce parents to cluster births more. Women whose wage rate rises more steeply with seniority of service or work experience (higher β) will tend to have their children later.

The conclusions that we have reached about the overall effects of A, K_M, e^0, and ϕ are not difficult to explain. Since children are assumed to be normal goods, and earlier children are assumed to give greater utility, other things being equal, than later ones, wealthier couples (or couples where the husband earns more) have more children, and sooner. A rise in the net set-up costs of a child, or a higher earning ability on the part of the wife, makes it more costly to increase the quantity of children, but not their quality, which depends on birth timing and above-subsistence expenditure. Therefore, a rise in the child-benefit rate results in higher completed fertility, but lower tempo, and higher-earning women have fewer children, but earlier in married life.

The explanation of the effects of α, ω, and r is slightly more subtle. The full cost of a child, normalized for quality, (p_t/v_t) must grow, it will be recalled, at the rate of interest. Therefore, if r rises, the growth rate of p_t must rise relative to that of v_t. Since p_t grows at the same rate as I_t, however, the only way to increase the difference between the growth rates of p_t and v_t is to put the whole birth calendar back—i.e. to lower the tempo of fertility.

By contrast a rise in ω would cause the opportunity-cost component (wage plus capital loss) of p_t to grow faster if the timing of births were not modified. Since the growth rate of I_t does not depend on ω, the growth rate of (p_t/v_t) would then rise. But that would not be optimal, because the

interest rate is still the same. Therefore, births must be so
redistributed in time that the growth rate of the opportunity
cost will stay the same despite the higher ω. A look at (8.11)
will persuade the reader that this can be done by lowering
the tempo of fertility: as a woman increases her labour
supply in the early years of marriage and reduces it in later
years, the rate of growth in her current wage rate becomes
lower, and the rate of decline in her capital loss higher, than
it would otherwise be.

Similar reasoning explains why the tempo of fertility
must be lower for women with higher β. Given the same
time distribution of births, the opportunity cost of having a
child would grow faster for these women than for women
whose wage rate rises less steeply with work experience.
However, the growth rate of (p_t/v_t) must be the same for all
women, because they all face the same rate of interest. In
order to achieve that equality, the opportunity cost of a
child must then grow more slowly for high-β than for low-β
women. Therefore, women in careers where the rate of
remuneration is strongly dependent on work experience
will tend to work more in the early part of marriage and to
have their children late.

8.3. *The Implications of Uncertainty*

The analysis so far has been based on the implicit assumption
that the economic environment and the outcome of fertility
decisions are not subject to uncertainty. The same was true,
of course, of the analysis of the preceding chapters. Ignoring
uncertainty seems, however, a less acceptable simplification
here where we are dealing with timing decisions: it is one
thing to say that a couple can decide to have two children in
total, another to say that they can decide to have one after
three years of marriage and the other after seven. It seems,
therefore, that the effect of uncertainty on decision-making
has to be taken explicitly into account.

Uncertainty, in the present context, takes two forms. One, which might be termed *technological uncertainty*, arises from the fact that a couple cannot control the timing of births with any degree of accuracy (they can always prevent a birth by efficient contraception, but cannot be sure of when exactly the birth will occur, even with the use of fertility drugs, if they do decide to have a child). The other is *market uncertainty*, arising from lack of complete information about the state of the economic environment at various future dates.

Faced with these uncertainties, a fully rational couple will make contingency plans. At the date of marriage, that is, they will plan an array of alternative courses of action for each future date, where each course of action is contingent on a particular state of the economic environment at that date, and on a particular sequence of actual outcomes of actions taken at earlier dates. That being the case, the probability distribution of a birth to any particular couple at any particular date would be conditioned not only by that couple's personal characteristics and by the state of the economic environment nine months before that date, but also by the entire fertility history of that couple, and by the history of the economic environment up to then.

Constructing a formal model of rational behaviour that takes account of both these forms of uncertainty is, however, extremely difficult in the present context. The relatively few attempts at constructing such a model[13] are based on drastic simplifications that remove much of the economic content. As a consequence of these simplifications, those theoretical models tend to have unrealistic bang-bang solutions, where the probability of childbirth is piled up either at the start of marriage or at the end of the mother's fecund life-span. Furthermore, these models tell us nothing about how the actual or the expected birth profile is affected by differences in personal characteristics, or by changes in the economic environment.

It seems, therefore, that all we have to go by, at this stage, is the kind of deterministic theory outlined in the last two sections, where parents are assumed to behave, on average, *as if* they operated in a world of complete certainty. In the next section we report on two empirical studies which throw some light on the reasonableness of that assumption.

8.4. *Two Empirical Studies*

Both studies[14] use the same set of micro-data, the *Women and Employment Survey*. That survey contains the marital, fertility, and employment histories of a large sample of British women who were between the ages of 16 and 59 in 1980. The data are illustrated by Figs. 8.1 to 8.3, which show the averaged fertility profiles, by duration of marriage to the same man, of various subsamples of women. It is interesting to note how the birth rate tends to fluctuate over married life around a downward trend, as predicted by the deterministic model examined earlier in this chapter. It is also noticeable how the pattern differs for women with different levels of education or work experience at the date of marriage, and for women in different types of occupation.

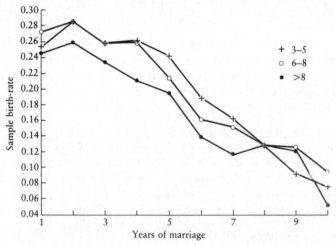

FIG. 8.1. Years of work experience at marriage
Source: Cigno and Ermisch (1989).

FIG. 8.2.   Last occupation before first birth
Source: Cigno and Ermisch (1989).

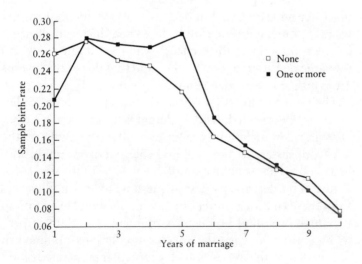

FIG. 8.3.   Years of post-compulsory education
Source: Cigno and Ermisch (1989).

Both studies relate the probability of having a child for any particular couple in any particular year of marriage to the woman's age at the date of marriage, to her work experience and level of education at marriage (both taken to be proxies of K_M), to her occupation before the birth of the first child (taken as a proxy for β), and to an estimate of the husband's lifetime income. The second of these two studies, however, allows the relationship to vary over married life according to the number of children actually born in previous years, thereby allowing for the fact that fertility cannot be perfectly controlled, and that the actions taken at any date will thus depend on the outcomes of past actions. Furthermore, it allows the probability of a birth at any date to depend on information about the economic environment (wage rates, child benefits) acquired since the date of marriage.

In other words, the later study[15] allows for the possibility that couples make contingency plans, and that their actions at any date depend, therefore, on information accrued up to that date, while the earlier study[16] models behaviour as if couples chose a particular sequence of actions at the date of marriage and stuck to that decision, come what may, for all years to come. It is remarkable, however, that even allowing for methodological differences[17] the two studies come to the same qualitative conclusions, and that these conclusions are consistent with deterministic theory.

The tentative hypothesis that emerges from these studies —yet to be verified with different sets of data—is that allowing for uncertainty does not alter the signs of the effects of differences in personal characteristics on fertility behaviour. That is quite remarkable in view of the sequential nature of the decision process in question. Indeed, it transpires from these empirical studies that, with one notable exception to which we shall come in a moment, the data appear to be consistent with the specific predictions obtained in Section 8.2 by the imposition of a particular parameterization and of special assumptions on the more general model of Section 8.1.

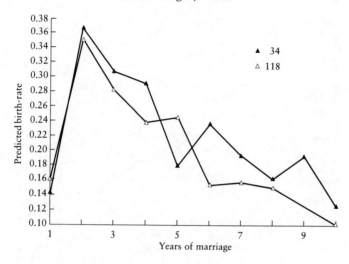

FIG. 8.4. Months of work experience at marriage
Source: Cigno and Ermisch (1989).

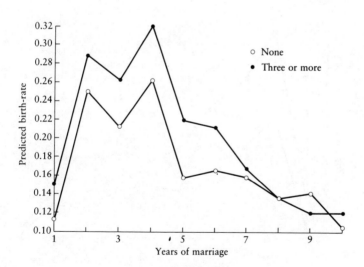

FIG. 8.5. Years of post-compulsory education
Source: Cigno and Ermisch (1989).

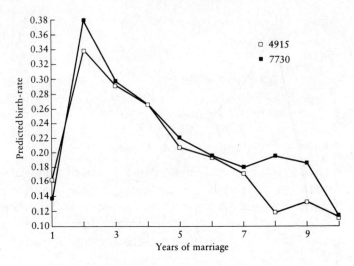

Fɪɢ. 8.6.   Husband's average annual earnings (1980 UK pounds)
Source: Cigno and Ermisch (1989).

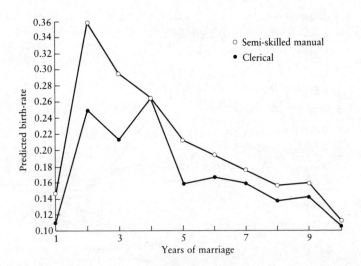

Fɪɢ. 8.7.   Last occupation before first birth
Source: Cigno and Ermisch (1989).

Figs. 8.4 to 8.7, reproduced from the earlier of the two studies, illustrate the estimated effects of differences in personal characteristics on the birth profile. Taking the number born by the tenth year of marriage as an indicator of completed fertility, and the proportion of that number falling within the first four years of marriage as an indicator of tempo, we can see that, as predicted by the theory, women with more human capital (greater education or work experience) at marriage, or with higher-earning husbands, have their children sooner, while women with steeper career profiles (those in clerical, as against manual, occupations) have their children later.

Much the same picture emerges from Fig. 8.8, drawn from the later study, which shows the estimated probability distribution of waiting time from marriage to first birth for a woman with the average number of years of education, and for a woman with one year more. Taking this waiting time as an (inverse) indicator of the tempo of fertility, we can see that better-educated women tend to have a higher tempo (their probability distribution is more skewed to the left).

Figs. 8.9 and 8.10, also drawn from the later study, show the estimated effects on the probability distribution of the waiting time to the first birth of, respectively, an increase in the average female wage rate (relative to the average male wage rate) and an increase in the benefit rate payable for the first child. While the wage rise lowers the tempo, as the theory predicts, the benefit rise, contrary to the theoretical prediction, raises the tempo. This divergence between theory and data[18] could be due to the fact that the waiting time to the first birth is only a very imperfect measure of tempo (if a couple delays the birth of the first child from the second to the third year of marriage but, at the same time, brings forward the birth of the second child from the sixth to the fifth year, is that a fall or a rise of tempo?). It must also be kept in mind that the theoretical prediction is specific to the particular parameterization and special assumptions used

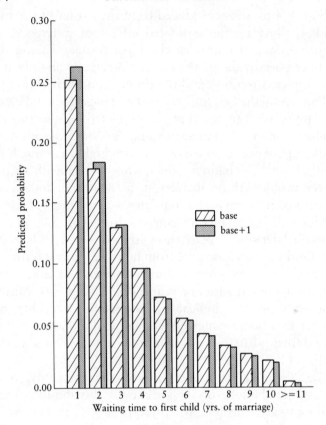

F IG. 8.8. Effect of increasing post-compulsory education by one year
Source: Barmby and Cigno (1990).

to make it. It would be enough that, in this particular
instance, the income effect dominated the substitution effect,
rather the other way round as assumed, for the benefit rate
to have a positive effect on tempo. None the less, we must
allow for the possibility that, where child benefits are
concerned, uncertainty does change the sign of the effect on
tempo.

An intuitive explanation of how uncertainty could make
that effect negative is based on the argument[19] that transfers
from the State are more certain than incomes derived from

market activities. Therefore, if the government announces a rise in the benefit rate for the year ahead, family plans involving a higher probability of childbearing in that year become less risky relative to plans involving higher probability of childbearing at later dates. A sufficiently risk-averse couple might then choose a plan that involves a high probability of a birth within the next twelve months in preference to one that involves a high probability of a birth later on (when child benefits are less certain to be so

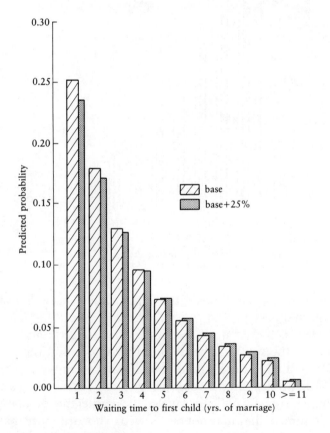

FIG. 8.9. Effect of increasing female wage rate (relative to male) by 25%
Source: Barmby and Cigno (1990).

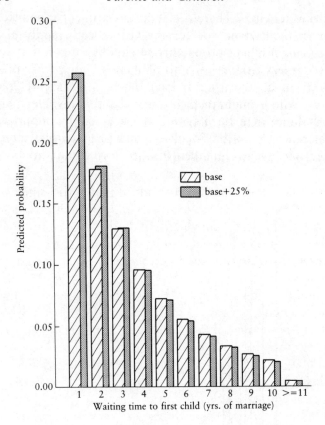

FIG. 8.10.   Effect of increasing the benefit rate by 25%
Source: Barmby and Cigno (1990).

generous), even though the latter might have a lower expected cost.

Here is an instance, therefore, where uncertainty could change the sign of a behavioural response. But, there is a different case, unrelated to parental uncertainty, in which the theoretical model could be 'wrong'. This is that, while couples can always lend (save) at the market rate of interest, as assumed, they may not be allowed to borrow more than a certain proportion of current earnings. A young couple with slender assets and still relatively low earnings might then face a liquidity constraint, because they might not be able to borrow as much as they would like, at the going interest rate, to finance the immediate birth of a child.[20] A rise in the benefit rate would relax that constraint. Therefore, if a sufficiently large proportion of young couples does not have enough assets to finance the desired birth profile, it could appear from the data that the tempo of fertility is positively related to the benefit rate.[21] However, the consistency with the data of the other theoretical predictions throws doubt on this liquidity-related explanation, and lends credibility to the uncertainty-related one.

8.5. *Fluctuations in the Period Birth Rate*

The theoretical and the empirical findings discussed in this chapter provide elements for explaining the sharp fluctuations in the *period birth rate* (number of births per unit of time, typically the year) that have characterized industrial societies since the end of the Second World War. These fluctuations cannot be attributed to movements of completed fertility, which has tended to fall steadily from one generation of women to the next,[22] but can be explained by the tempo moving in the opposite direction from completed fertility, or actually fluctuating.[23] Indeed, in a situation where most couples want only one or two children in, say, 20–5 fecund years of married life, there is plenty of scope for changes of tempo.

The baby boom of the 1960s, for example, was the outcome of the rise in the tempo of fertility over the 50s and 60s, and subsequent fall at the start of the 70s. What caused those changes of tempo? Three major changes took place, over the period in question, in the factors affecting a woman's participation in the labour market. One was the rapid increase in the amount of education received by women (more rapid than the corresponding increase for men, who started from a higher level). This will have had a positive effect on the tempo of fertility through its positive effect on human capital. The other two were the increase in labour productivity (through technical progress) and the mitigation of sexual discrimination. Both these developments will have tended to raise the rate of return to human capital. The lessening of sexual discrimination, furthermore, opened up opportunities to enter careers which women had previously found it difficult or impossible to pursue. Both these developments (corresponding to rises in β and ω) will have had a negative effect on tempo. All we have to hypothesize, in order to explain the fluctuation, is then that the positive effect on tempo of increasing female education predominated in the two earlier decades, as young women were still catching up with their male counterparts, while the negative effects, particularly that of diminishing discrimination, became predominant at the start of the 70s (when some countries also passed legislation to that end). Changes in child benefit and tax regimes may also have played a part, particularly in explaining why the fluctuation was sharper in some countries than in others. However, since the phenomenon occurred more or less at the same time in so many different countries, it seems unlikely that local policy changes could have actually been the *cause* of the fluctuation.

These fluctuations of the annual birth rate are a source of great concern for governments, because the associated fluctuations in the demand for places in maternity hospitals and schools put undesirable strains on the provision of such services (which cannot be expanded and contracted quickly). Furthermore, they cause budgetary difficulties for pay-as-you-go pension systems (as all public pension systems essentially are) which finance current old-age pensions out of the contributions paid by those currently in work. A sudden drop in the number of births will in fact cause, twenty or so years later, a drop in the ratio of payers to beneficiaries of the pension system.[24]

Governments should thus be interested not only in predicting, but also in controlling these fluctuations. Here, too, the preceding analysis is of some use. If a government were concerned to stop or reverse the tendency to delay motherhood, which has prevailed throughout Western Europe and the industrialized world generally since the 70s, that government could make the tax treatment of married women's earnings less favourable (i.e. reduce ω).[25] The orientation of fiscal policy in some parts of Western Europe appears, however, to be the exact opposite. In an attempt to expand the tax base out of which public pension systems draw their financial resources, governments have been trying to stimulate labour-market participation by all, but particularly by married women, whose labour supply is the most responsive to net wage changes (see Chapters 2 and 7). That policy may well be doomed to failure because, by encouraging potential mothers to supply more labour, it is likely to induce further falls in the annual birth rate (partly through a further decline of completed fertility, partly through a further fall in tempo) and thus to worsen the budgetary problems of public pension systems it is supposed to cure.[26] Such are the hazards of taking fertility as exogenous.

NOTES

1. In their analysis of US National Longitudinal Surveys of Labor Market Experience, Calhoun and Espenshade (1988) note that, 'while 50 per cent of the impact of each child on forgone lifetime hours of market work occurs within the first five years following the birth of the child [the] effect on forgone earnings is more prolonged . . . It takes roughly ten years following a birth before 50 per cent of the total impact of each child on forgone market earnings is realised . . .'.
2. The analysis that follows draws on Cigno (1988b, 1989). Earlier studies tried to capture aspects of the timing decision within an essentially static framework. Razin (1980) postulates that parents choose the number of, and average interval between, births under the assumption that the quality of the average child increases with the average length of that interval. Schultz (1976) and Lee (1980) use a stock-adjustment model in which the speed of adjustment to the

140   *Parents and Children*

desired quantity of children is not derived from intertemporal optimization.

3. We are ignoring the other 'physiological' restriction that, for any one couple, B_t can only be zero or a whole number. The same was true, of course, of n in the last chapter, but the omission is more visible here, because we are looking at the distribution of n over several fecund years of marriage. The model should thus be interpreted as a description of the average behaviour of a large number of couples (whose individual behaviour is differentiated as a result of differences in personal characteristics and circumstances which do not figure in the model).

4. In the same way as we implicitly assume the preferences and market conditions portrayed in the model to be such that a solution will not include unrealistic values of C_t and I_t (C_t less than subsistence, I_t negative), we might also assume those preferences and market conditions to be such that, even without (8.7), the solution would not include values of B_t lower than zero or higher than nature permits. The last of these assumptions, namely that the physiological ceiling on B_t is never binding, will not be applicable to every couple, but seems appropriate if the model is supposed to describe average behaviour. For example, in the statistical survey of British women referred to later in this chapter, the annual birth rate (of the sample as a whole, and of various subsamples of women with common characteristics) is never found to be as low as zero or as high as one-third—well inside the physiological limits—for any of the first ten years of marriage.

5. Cigno (1983*b*) simplifies the derivation by assuming that the quality of children is a constant, so that the choice of birth profile is determined by financial considerations only. Happel *et al.* (1984) takes the profile of births after the first as given, so that the choice of timing reduces to a choice of waiting time to the first birth. Moffitt (1984*b*) and Rosenzweig and Schultz (1985) assume the whole profile to be determined by non-economic factors.

6. Evidence to this effect is reported in Calhoun and Espenshade (1988).

7. Since, as we shall see in a moment, this is what appears to happen in reality, it is interesting that we can explain the phenomenon without recourse to an assumption of economies of scale in child rearing which does not seem to have empirical support (see Chap. 6).

8. A model similar to ours, Moffitt (1984*a*), appears to have run into the same problem.

9. Furthermore, the values of the other parameters must be such that B_t is not chosen negative for any t.

10. See Cigno (1988*b*, 1989) for detailed derivations.
11. See Cigno (1988*b*, 1989).
12. This is overlooked in Cigno (1988*b*, 1989).
13. See, for example, Newman (1983), Hotz and Miller (1986).
14. Cigno and Ermisch (1989), Barmby and Cigno (1990).
15. See Barmby and Cigno (1990).
16. Cigno and Ermisch (1989).
17. Cigno and Ermisch (1989) estimate an ordered probit model, while Barmby and Cigno (1990) fit a logit function.
18. Confirmed by a separate time-series analysis, Ermisch (1987*b*), which also shows a negative effect, in Britain, of the benefit rate on the waiting time to the first birth.
19. Barmby and Cigno (1990).
20. While unrelated to parental uncertainty, this explanation has still to do with uncertainty—that of the lenders of funds to aspiring parents.
21. That need not be so if differences in asset holdings are controlled for, but that could not be done in the studies quoted, because the survey does not contain information on assets.
22. In Italy, for example, completed fertility was 2.11 for women born in 1939–40, 2.07 for women born in 1944–5, and 1.89 for those born in 1949–50. In England and Wales, it was 2.37 for 1939–40, 2.22 for 1944–5, 2.04 for 1949–50. In West Germany, it was 1.98, 1.79, and 1.72, respectively; in France, 2.42, 2.25, and 2.14. See Hopflinger (1984).
23. In Italy, while completed fertility was falling, the proportion of completed fertility realized before age 25 rose from 31 per cent for the generation of women born in 1939–40, to 37 per cent for that born in 1944–5, to 39 per cent for that of 1949–50. In the other larger West European countries, there was first a rise and then a fall. In England and Wales, from 44 per cent for the 1939–40 generation, to 48 for that of 1944–5, to 46 for that of 1949–50. In France, from 44 to 49, to 46. See Hopflinger (1984); also Muñoz-Perez (1986).
24. We come back to this issue in Chap. 10.
25. More generous child benefits (higher ϕ) *might* also help, though the sign of their effect on tempo is in doubt, in the light of earlier discussion, and there would also be undesirable side-effects on the quality of children (see Chapter 7).
26. See Cigno (1990*b*) for a fuller discussion.

9

Intergenerational Issues

In the foregoing analysis of parental decisions we allowed for the possibility that the flow of resources between generations might not be all one way. In particular, we noted in Chapter 6 that the commodity component of the cost of a child could be the algebraic sum of two flows of opposite sign: one from the parents to the child when the child is young, the other from the child to the parents when the parents are old. The same may be said about the time component of the cost of a child: parents spend time caring for their young children, but some grown-up children also spend time caring for elderly parents.

As the focus of the last three chapters was the determination of reproductive decisions, all that mattered, there, were net flows. The fine detail of the balance-sheet seemed unimportant. It becomes important in the present chapter, however, as the focus of the analysis shifts from reproduction to the network of transactions that different generations entertain with one another.

9.1. *The Family as a Substitute for the Capital Market*

Suppose that every person lives for three periods of equal duration. Let us call the first period 'youth', the second 'middle age', and the third 'old age'. Suppose, also, for now, that people are selfish, meaning that they derive utility from their own consumption only. We shall drop this assumption later in the chapter, but we want to see, first, how much of family members' behaviour can be explained by self-interest alone. Denoting by c_i^t the consumption in the ith period of life ($i = 1,2,3$) of a person born at date t, we can then write the utility of such a person as

$$U^t = U(c_1^t, c_2^t, c_3^t). \qquad (9.1)$$

Let us also suppose that income in middle age is higher than income in each of the other two periods (e.g. because of life-cycle changes in productivity).

Under the usual assumption that $U(\ )$ is quasi-concave, utility will be higher if there is a way for each person to transfer purchasing power from the middle to the other two ages of his or her life. If there is a capital market, that can be accomplished by borrowing and lending on that market.[1] Suppose, however, that there is no such market, or that, for whatever reason (e.g. lack of knowledge, or prohibitive transaction costs) the people in question do not have access to it. Suppose, also, that anyone who has children has them at the start of middle age. An extended family network inclusive of three generations at different stages of life could then substitute for the market by arranging loans from its middle-aged to its young members, and enforcing the repayment of those loans one period later, when the young borrowers have become middle-aged and the middle-aged lenders have become old.

How are the terms of these intra-family loans determined? Bargaining between parents and children is not unknown in real life, but it would not make sense to assume that children, the moment they are born, have to actually negotiate a loan with their parents (or other middle-aged relatives) in order to survive. We may suppose, on the other hand, that the family in its collective wisdom sets rules of conduct, such that no member would be better off without the family than within. Let us see what these rules might be.

Suppose, for simplicity, that every person receives a certain amount of perishable commodities, which we shall call *income*, in middle age, but nothing at all in the other two periods of life. Consumption in the first period of life of anyone born at t must then come out of the income of someone born at $(t - 1)$. Conversely, consumption in the third period of life of someone born at t must come out of the income of someone born at $(t + 1)$. Let y^t and d^t denote, respectively, the income received and the amount transferred to the old, during middle age, by a member of generation t (i.e. by someone born at t). Denote by n^t the ratio of the number of family members born at $(t + 1)$ to that born at t (i.e. the number of children per head in generation t). Then, we shall have that

$$c_2^t + d^t + c_1^{t+1}\, n^t = y^t \tag{9.2}$$

and

$$c_3^t = d^{t+1}\, n^t \tag{9.3}$$

for each t. Since n^t is the completed fertility (expressed in per-capita, rather than per-woman, terms) of generation t, there will also be a physiological restriction,

$$0 \leqslant n^t \leqslant m, \tag{9.4}$$

for each t.

In the circumstances described, it seems reasonable to suppose that the family rules would prescribe c_1^t and d^t for each t. Define

$$\rho^t \equiv \frac{d^t}{c_1^t}. \tag{9.5}$$

Then, the implicit rate of interest on intra-family loans at date t, and the rate of return to having a child for generation $(t - 1)$, is $(\rho^t - 1)$. Using (9.5) to substitute for d^t in (9.2) and d^{t+1} in (9.3), and (9.3) to substitute for n^t in (9.2), we obtain

$$c_1^t + \frac{c_2^t}{\rho^t} + \frac{c_3^t}{\rho^t \rho^{t+1}} = \frac{y^t}{\rho^t}. \tag{9.6}$$

This looks like the lifetime budget constraint of a consumer with access to a competitive capital market where the interest rate is $(\rho^t - 1)$ at date t, $(\rho^{t+1} - 1)$ at date $(t + 1)$, etc.

If there really were such a market, and if it were possible

for everyone to trade in that market right from birth, anyone born at t would borrow, in the first period of life, to the point where the marginal rate of substitution of c_1^t for c_2^t equals the interest factor ruling at t,

$$\frac{U_1^t}{U_2^t} = \rho^t. \tag{9.7}$$

and lend, in the second period of life, to the point where the marginal rate of substitution of c_2^t for c_3^t equals the interest factor ruling at $(t+1)$,

$$\frac{U_2^t}{U_3^t} = \rho^{t+1}. \tag{9.8}$$

This gives us a clue as to how the family rules have to be set. Note that (9.5), (9.7), and (9.8) imply

$$\frac{U_2^{t-1}}{U_3^{t-1}} = \frac{U_1^t}{U_2^t} = \frac{d^t}{c_1^t}. \tag{9.9}$$

Let $\{\bar{c}_1^t, \bar{d}^t, \bar{n}^t\}$ be a sequence of combinations of values of c_1^t, d^t, and n^t satisfying (9.2)–(9.4) and (9.9) for each t. If the family rules prescribed to generation t the transfers levels $\bar{c}_1^{t+1}$ and $\bar{d}^t$, each member of that generation would then maximize his or her utility by choosing $c_2^t = \bar{c}_2^t$, $c_3^t = \bar{c}_3^t$ and, therefore, $n^t = (c_3^t/d^{t+1}) = \bar{n}^t$. Furthermore, had it been able to decide how much to borrow in its youth at the implied rate of interest $[(\bar{d}^t/\bar{c}_1^t) - 1]$, generation t would have chosen $c_1^t = \bar{c}_1^t$. Of course, generation t would rather *not* pay $\bar{d}^t$ to generation $(t-1)$. However, since everyone needs the family framework in order to survive in old age, the prospect of expulsion from the family fold will deter any member from disobeying the rules.

Once established, and whatever its rationale at the time, any set of rules consistent with (9.2)–(9.4) and (9.9) for each t will tend to persist until there is an external change of circumstances. Even though each generation would like to borrow at as low a rate of interest as possible when young, and lend at as high a rate of interest as possible when middle-aged, it must in fact be remembered that the interest rate at which a generation lends is the interest rate at which the next generation has to borrow. Therefore, no generation would acquiesce to a change of rules that raised its repayments to the previous generation, or lowered the return on its loans to the next one. Indeed (9.9) are the first-order conditions for a Pareto-optimum constrained by (9.2)–(9.4). It is not possible, therefore, to devise a different method of bringing sustenance to the young and to the old that would make any generation better off without making some other generation worse off.

9.2. The Capital Market as a Substitute for the Family

Let us now suppose that the family has access to the capital market. If we assume that nobody outside the family would lend to a young person,[2] the existence of such a market does not eliminate the family's role as a reallocator of consumption over the life-cycle of its members. It does, however, put a floor below the rate of interest on intra-family loans. Since the middle-aged have the choice of lending to the market or to their young relatives, it is in fact clear that the domestic rate of interest must be at least as high as the market rate. But that is not high enough.[3]

Take any generation t. At date $(t + 1)$, its members, now middle-aged, will have already consumed the amount $\bar{c}_1^t$ 'borrowed' from generation $(t - 1)$. If they paid back that loan and, at the same time, 'lent' to the next family generation at the domestic rate of interest $(\rho^{t+1} - 1)$, their budget constraint at that date would be

$$c_2^t + \frac{c_3^t}{\rho^{t+1}} = y^t - \bar{d}^t. \tag{9.10}$$

If, on the other hand, they did not pay anything to the old, and lent to the market at the commercial rate of interest $(r^{t+1} - 1)$, their budget constraint would be

$$c_2^t + \frac{c_3^t}{r^{t+1}} = y^t. \tag{9.11}$$

If ρ^{t+1} had been set equal to r^{t+1}, the generation that reached middle age at date $(t + 1)$ would clearly be better off under (9.11) than under (9.10). As a consequence, since the threat of expulsion is no longer a deterrent against disobeying family rules (because it is now possible to provide for one's own old age by lending to the market) selfish middle-aged people would default on their obligations to elderly relatives. To prevent that happening, the rate of interest on intra-family loans must then be set high enough to make each middle-aged member at least as well off under family rule, as he or she would be standing alone. The determination of the lowest value of ρ^{t+1} that will do that for generation t is illustrated in Fig. 9.1. It is equal to the absolute slope of the straight line with intercept on the c_2-

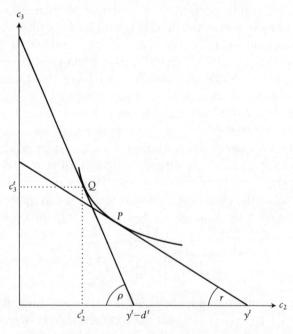

Fig. 9.1.

axis $(y^t - \bar{d}^t)$, that is tangent to the same indifference curve as the straight line with absolute slope r^{t+1} and intercept y^t. The domestic interest rate is, therefore, always higher than the market rate.[4]

For each t, ρ^{t+1} must then satisfy

$$V(c_1^t, y^t, r^{t+1}) \leqslant V[c_1^t, (y^t - d^t), \rho^{t+1}], \qquad (9.12)$$

where the term on the left denotes the value of U^t maximized subject to (9.11), and that on the right the value of U^t maximized subject to (9.10), for any given c_1^t, d^t, y^t, and r^{t+1}. This additional constraint may not be binding, i.e. the rate of interest implicit in the family rules could be higher than is strictly required to keep the middle-aged in line. On the other hand, (9.12) might not be consistent with the physiological constraint (9.4). In other words, it might not be possible to find a domestic rate of interest (for some or for all t) high enough to satisfy (9.12) because the associated fertility level would be too high to satisfy (9.4).

By way of illustration, consider the case where

$$U(c_1^t, c_2^t, c_3^t) \equiv c_1^{\alpha_1}\, c_2^{\alpha_2}\, c_3^{\alpha_3}, \ \alpha_i > 0, \ \Sigma_i \alpha_i = 1. \qquad (9.13)$$

Suppose that the family rules stipulate that the domestic rate of interest must be the lowest possible, i.e. that (9.12) must hold as an equation for all t. Suppose, also, that income and the market rate of interest are constant ($y^t = y$ and $r^t = r$ for all t). If the physiological constraint (9.4) is not binding, the system has a steady-state solution (i.e. one where c_i^t, d^t, ρ^t, and n^t are the same at all t):

$$\bar{c}_1 \equiv \alpha_1\, \alpha\, \frac{y}{r}, \qquad (9.14)$$

$$\bar{c}_2 \equiv \alpha_2\, y, \qquad (9.15)$$

$$\bar{c}_3 \equiv \frac{\alpha_3}{\alpha} y, \qquad (9.16)$$

$$\bar{d} \equiv \alpha_1\, y, \qquad (9.17)$$

$$\bar{n} \equiv \frac{\alpha_3}{\alpha_1 \alpha} r \qquad (9.18)$$

and

$$\bar{\rho} \equiv \frac{r}{\alpha}, \tag{9.19}$$

where

$$\alpha \equiv (\alpha_2 + \alpha_3)^{\frac{\alpha_2 + \alpha_3}{\alpha_3}} \tag{9.20}$$

is clearly less than unity. In this example, the family rules have a particularly simple form: transfers to the old are a fixed proportion of income, and transfers to the young are the present value of transfers to the old.

Notice that, in our example, the domestic rate of interest rises with the market rate.[5] The reason for that is clear from Fig. 9.1, and does not depend on the particular form of the utility function. Notice, further, that the consumption of the old rises, and the consumption of the young falls, as the market and the domestic rates of interest go up. That, too, is independent of the particular form of the utility function. Since, in the absence of altruism, nobody is allowed to be a net lifetime borrower (the amount borrowed in youth must be paid back in middle age), and nobody has any wish to be a net lifetime lender (i.e. of transferring assets to future generations) interest rate changes have, in fact, no income effect. Therefore, the overall effect of ρ on c_1 will be a pure substitution effect, and that on c_3 a pure cross-substitution effect.

In our example, we also found a positive relationship between fertility and the market rate of interest, but that may not be true in general. To see this, recall that n^t is equal to the ratio between c_3^t and d^{t+1}, and that d^{t+1}, in turn, is equal to $c_1^{t+1} \rho^{t+1}$. If preferences are *homothetic* (indifference curves parallel along any radial from the origin), as in (9.13), $c_1^{t+1} \rho^{t+1}$ does not vary with ρ^{t+1}. Therefore, as c_3^t and ρ^{t+1} rise with r^{t+1}, so does n^t. In general, however, a rise in r^{t+1} could cause $c_1^{t+1} \rho^{t+1}$ to increase and, thus, have an ambiguous effect on n^t.

Be that as it may, if n^t increases with ρ^{t+1}, as r^{t+1} rises, the physiological constraint (9.4) will set an upper bound on ρ^{t+1}, as well as on n^t, and may thus be incompatible with (9.12). As a consequence, if the market rate of interest rises to a high level, the domestic rate might not be able to rise sufficiently to stay competitive, because that could entail a number of children per head greater than the physiological maximum, m. Should that unexpectedly happen, the old—who had been counting on their children's support—would starve.

If, on the other hand, it had been known all along that such an interest rate rise was going to occur at date t, generation $(t-2)$ would have guarded against the consequences of such an event by lending to the market, at date $(t-1)$, instead of lending to generation $(t-1)$. But, then, generation $(t-2)$ would have had no reason to have children. Therefore, there would have been no generation $(t-1)$. Furthermore, generation $(t-2)$ would have paid nothing to the old of generation $(t-3)$. Had generation $(t-3)$ foreseen that, it too would have made provision for its own old age through the market, and would have had no children. Therefore, there would have been no generation $(t-2)$ either, and so on. In conclusion, if the family credit network is expected to break down at some point in the future, it will be shunned from the start in favour of the market alternative. In that case, the first generation of the family will also be its last.

The opening of a capital market offering an interest rate so high that the family network cannot compete (again because it cannot produce enough children) has similar, but not identical, consequences to an unmatchable interest-rate rise in an existing market. One difference is that the opening of a capital market, being outside the range of experience of the family members concerned, is less likely to be foreseen than an interest-rate rise. Therefore, it is likely that a family unaccustomed to conduct its intertemporal transactions through the market will go on happily reproducing itself until one generation unexpectedly finds, in its old age, that the next generation is unwilling to pay back the loans received. The other difference is that, even if the opening of the market were anticipated, there is nothing that anyone could have done to avoid its consequences because, until the market is open, there is no alternative to relying on filial support for old age. Therefore, not even the first (and last) generation of the family will have any means of transferring purchasing power from middle to old age.

All this has been based on the assumption that parents could, if they so chose, spend nothing for their children.[6] Let us now assume, instead, that some minimum cost γ^t has to be incurred, say by law, if a child is born at t. As in previous chapters, we shall take it that this minimum cost includes, among other things, the child's subsistence consumption in the first period of life.

Redefining c_1^t as youthful consumption over and above the minimum included in γ^t by someone born at t, (9.2) becomes

$$c_2^t + d^t + (\gamma^{t+1} + c_1^{t+1})n^t = y^t. \qquad (9.21)$$

Accordingly, the domestic interest factor at t is

$$\rho^t \equiv \frac{d^t}{\gamma^t + c_1^t}, \qquad (9.22)$$

and the lifetime budget constraint of generation t may be written as

$$c_1^t \rho^t + c_2^t + c_3^t \rho^{t+1} = y^t - \gamma^t \rho^t. \qquad (9.23)$$

The introduction of this fixed element in the cost of a child modifies the rule for shifting consumption over the life-cycle, (9.9), which becomes

$$\frac{U_2^{t-1}}{U_3^{t-1}} = \frac{U_1^t}{U_2^t} = \frac{d^t}{\gamma^t + c_1^t}. \qquad (9.24)$$

Furthermore, it gives rise to an inverse relationship between the size of the budget, i.e. the right-hand side of (9.23), and the domestic rate of interest. Therefore, as ρ^t rises, c_1^t will still fall, but c_2^t will fall too, and c_3^t may not rise. The direction of the change in n^t remains ambiguous in general.

In the special case where the utility function is (9.13), the steady-state solution is

$$\bar{c}_1 = \alpha_1 \, \frac{y - \gamma\bar{\rho}}{\bar{\rho}}, \tag{9.25}$$

$$\bar{c}_2 = \alpha_2 \, (y - \gamma\bar{\rho}), \tag{9.26}$$

$$\bar{c}_3 = \alpha_3 \, (y - \gamma\bar{\rho})\bar{\rho}, \tag{9.27}$$

$$\bar{d} = \gamma\bar{\rho} + \alpha_1 \, (y - \gamma\bar{\rho}), \tag{9.28}$$

and

$$\bar{n} = \frac{\alpha_3 \, (y - \gamma\bar{\rho})\bar{\rho}}{\gamma\bar{\rho} + \alpha_1 \, (y - \gamma\bar{\rho})}, \tag{9.29}$$

with $\bar{\rho}$ still given by (9.19). It can be easily verified, by differentiating with respect to $\bar{\rho}$, that the steady-state relationships between consumption at various ages and the rate of interest are as indicated for the general case. The number of children, however, definitely increases with r and e. Therefore, we have still the problem that the domestic credit network may not be able to compete with the market at high rates of interest—with the implications that we have already discussed.

This is consistent with the observation that the growth of the financial sector (including in that the social security system, as well as banks, private insurance, and the stock exchange) tends to coincide, in the development of an economy, with a sharp fall in fertility, the break-up of extended family networks, and a widespread reluctance on the part of the middle-aged to accept responsibility for the maintenance of elderly relatives. The fact that fertility does not actually fall to zero, even for couples who make little or no contribution to the welfare of elderly parents (and must, therefore, realistically expect the same treatment from their own children), suggests, however, that the demand for children is not entirely derived from the demand for old-age consumption. In other words, we need to assume that, for some couples at least, children enter the utility function of their parents in some form in order to explain why children are raised even when they are not required for old-age security purposes.

9.3. *Altruism towards Children*

It is thus time to reintroduce some decent human feelings in family relationships. We start by going back to the hypothesis of the last two chapters, that parents derive utility from the quantity and quality of children. We retain, however, all the life-cycle assumptions made in this chapter. People thus have two motives—one selfish, the other altruistic —for having children and for transferring resources to them. Let us see what difference that makes.

Identifying the quality of children born to generation t with the utility of a member of generation $(t + 1)$, the utility of a member of generation t will be given by

$$U^t = U(c_1^t, c_2^t, c_3^t, n^t, U^{t+1}), \tag{9.30}$$

where the function $U(\ )$ is again assumed to be increasing and quasi-concave in all its arguments. Since, in turn,

$$U^{t+1} = U(c_1^{t+1}, c_2^{t+1}, c_3^{t+1}, n^{t+1}, U^{t+2}), \tag{9.31}$$

and so on, the utility of each generation depends, ultimately, on the consumption stream and completed fertility of all subsequent generations, as well as its own. Thus, we may write the utility of the first generation of the family as

$$U^0 = W(c_1^0, c_2^0, c_3^0, n^0; c_1^1, c_2^1, c_3^1, n^1; c_1^2, c_2^2, c_3^2, n^2; \ldots), \tag{9.32}$$

that of the second as

$$U^1 = W(c_1^1, c_2^1, c_3^1, n^1; c_1^2, c_2^2, c_3^2, n^2; c_1^3, c_2^3, c_3^3, n^3; \ldots), \tag{9.33}$$

and so on.

Let us then put ourselves in the shoes of generation 0, which we may wish to think of as consisting of just one couple: the founders of our dynasty. By date 1, when generation 0 is at an age of making expenditure and fertility decisions, c_1^0 is already gone. Let us also take d^0 as given—

determined by events that occurred before our story began —and assume that there is no capital market. Being altruistic towards its descendants, generation 0 will be concerned not only about $(c_2^0, c_3^0, n^0, c_1^1)$, but also about $(c_2^1, c_3^1, n^1, c_1^2)$, $(c_2^2, c_3^2, n^2, c_1^3)$, etc. Indeed, it will want that sequence of expenditure and fertility plans to maximize (9.32), subject to the feasibility constraints (9.2)–(9.3)–(9.4) for $t = 0, 1, 2,$ . . . Will subsequent generations carry out those plans?

There are two problems here. One is that, as parents care about their children, but children do not care about their parents, each generation would rather not pay anything to the previous generation. The other is that, although preferences are assumed to be the same in each generation, preferences may not be *time-consistent*. In other words, although attitudes to children and grandchildren do not change from one generation to the other, any generation t may still wish to treat generation $(t + 1)$ differently from how generation $(t - 1)$ had thought desirable, because the members of generation $(t + 1)$ are the children of generation t, but the grandchildren of generation $(t - 1)$.

The first of these problems is, of course, the same as the one we encountered earlier in this chapter, when we were assuming total lack of altruism. As in Section 9.1, we may then take it for granted that fear of exclusion from the family transfer network will deter any member of any generation from defaulting on repayments to the previous generation. The second problem could be dealt with by assuming time-consistency, but that would impose severe restrictions on the possible form that the utility function can take. All of this also applies, of course, to the implementation of the plans made by generation 1, generation 2, and so on.

Does it make a difference if the family has access to the capital market? If that is the case, the constraints (9.2) and (9.3) cease to be relevant because, as we saw in the last section, it is possible to provide for one's own old age by 'saving' (i.e. lending to the market) during middle age. Indeed, given altruism towards future generations, we may well find that a generation will save more than it needs to finance its planned old-age consumption, because it wants to make bequests or gifts *inter vivos*[7] to the next generation. For this reason, we shall find it more convenient to conduct the analysis in terms of the negative of d^t,

$$b^t \equiv -d^t. \tag{9.34}$$

In place of (9.2) and (9.3), each generation faces now the constraint that the sum of the present values, discounted at the market rates of interest, of its own and its descendants' expenditures, minus the sum of the present values, similarly discounted, of its own and its descendants' incomes, must be equal to the sum of any transfers received from the previous generation. Thus, for generation 0,

$$\sum_{t=0}^{\infty} \left[\frac{N^t}{R^t}(c_2^t - y^t) + \frac{N^t c_3^t}{R^{t+1}} + \frac{N^{t+1}}{R^t}(\gamma^{t+1} + c_1^{t+1}) \right] = b^0,$$

$$\tag{9.35}$$

where

$$N^0 \equiv 1, \quad N^t \equiv \pi_{j=0}^{t-1} \, n^j \tag{9.36}$$

and

$$R^0 \equiv 1, \quad R^t \equiv \pi_{j=0}^{t} \, r^i. \tag{9.37}$$

If it could dictate to its successors, generation 0 would then choose $(c_2^t, c_3^t, n^t, c_1^{t+1})$, for $t = 0, 1, 2, \ldots$, so as to maximize (9.32), subject to the dynastic budget constraint (9.35), with b^0 given, and to the physiological restriction (9.4) for $t = 0, 1, 2, \ldots$ But, compliance by future generations cannot be taken for granted. First, we have that the value of b^t desired by generation 0, although probably positive for most t, may be negative for some t. If y^{t-1} is abnormally low, for example, the family founders might wish generation $(t-1)$ to be supported in old age by generation t. If that happens, generation t will not want to comply with the wishes of generation 0. Furthermore, it would not be possible to persuade generation t to give to generation $(t-1)$ in exchange for being allowed to charge its children a higher interest rate than the market (as in the model without altruism of the last section), because generation t cares about its own children. Altruism to children thus makes people behave worse, if anything, towards their own parents!

Instead of the constraint (9.12), discussed in the last section, generation 0 will then face the more stringent requirement that transfers cannot be negative,

$$b^t \geqslant 0 \qquad (9.38)$$

for $t = 1,2,3, \ldots$. Even if these constraints are satisfied, however, the sequence of expenditure and fertility plans favoured by generation 0 may not be implemented because preferences may not be time-consistent.[8] The same can again be said about the implementation of plans made by generation 1, generation 2, etc.

9.4. *Altruism towards Parents*

We have seen that the introduction of altruism towards children makes it paradoxically more difficult to establish rules of family conduct to which every generation will acquiesce. This difficulty disappears if we suppose that altruism extends backwards, towards parents and grandparents, as well as forward, towards children and grandchildren. If that is the case, $W(\ )$ may be interpreted as the utility function common to all family members, and the value of the right-hand side of (9.32) as the level of the utility of each member of each generation. There will be, then, total concordance of views within the dynastic family.

If the family does not have access to the capital market, the sequence of consumption and fertility levels adopted by successive generations will satisfy

$$\frac{W_1^t}{W_2^t} = \rho^t \qquad (9.39)$$

for $t = 1,2,3, \ldots$, and

$$\frac{W_2^t}{W_3^t} = \rho^{t+1} \tag{9.40}$$

for $t = 0,1,2, \ldots$, where W_i^t denotes the marginal utility of c_i^t. Furthermore, for $t = 0,1,2, \ldots$, we shall either have that n^t equals the physiological maximum, m, or that

$$\frac{W_n^t}{W_2^t} = \gamma^{t+1} + c_1^{t+1} - \frac{d^{t+1}}{\rho t}, \tag{9.41}$$

where W_n^t denotes the marginal utility of n^t.

On the face of it, (9.39) and (9.40) look very much like (9.7) and (9.8) in that they equate the marginal rate of substitution of consumption at various points in the life of generation t to the appropriate domestic interest factor. The difference is that in (9.7) and (9.8) the marginal rates of substitution are those of generation t and no one else, while in (9.39) and (9.40) they are also those of every other generation in the family. That is so, of course, because (9.7) and (9.8) are derived under the assumption that no one cares about anyone else, while (9.39) and (9.40) descend from the assumption that everyone in the family cares about everyone else.

For that same reason, (9.41) does not have a counterpart under the assumption of no altruism. The equivalent of (9.41) is the condition (7.14) that governs the number of children in the model of parental altruism examined in Chapter 7. Like (7.14), (9.41) equates the net cost of a child to the marginal rate of substitution of quantity of children for parental consumption. However, the marginal valuation of number of children figuring on the left of (7.14) is that of the parents of the children in question, and need not be shared by any other family member, while that on the left of (9.41) represents the unanimous judgement of all family members, past, present and future.

Another important difference between the present situation and that of no altruism is that, here, the domestic interest rates cannot be fixed arbitrarily. They come out of the maximization of (9.32) subject to (9.2)–(9.3)–(9.4) for $t = 0,1,2, \ldots$ Furthermore, as is clear from (9.41), ρ^t is, in the present case, *larger* than $[d^t/\gamma^t + c_1^t)]$, because the commodity equivalent of the utility that parents and every other family member would derive from having an extra child (i.e. the marginal rate of substitution of n^{t-1} for c_2^{t-1}) must be subtracted from the cost of the child.

If the family does have access to the capital market, the domestic rate of interest is equated to the market rate,

$$\rho^t = r^t. \tag{9.42}$$

Furthermore, there is a change in the condition governing the number of children to be raised by generation t (if the physiological constraint is not binding), which now becomes

$$\frac{W_n^t}{W_2^t} = \gamma^{t+1} + \frac{c^{t+1} - y^{t+1}}{r^{t+1}}, \tag{9.43}$$

where

$$c^{t+1} \equiv c_1^{t+1} r^{t+1} + c_2^{t+1} + \frac{c_3^{t+1}}{r^{t+2}} \tag{9.44}$$

is the lifetime consumption expenditure, evaluated at date $(t + 2)$, of a family member born at date $(t + 1)$. That is because, as the sequence of constraints (9.2)–(9.3)–(9.4) is replaced by the intergenerational budget constraint (9.35), it becomes possible for the family to swap expenditures between any two points in its history. Thus, the benefit of an extra birth in any generation is now equated to the net cost of the child for the dynasty as a whole (i.e. to the difference between cost and earnings), and not just to the net cost for the parents. Since the term on the left of (9.43) is positive, the net cost of a child is positive whenever the number of births is not pressing against the physiological ceiling. As in the model of Chapter 7, therefore, a child is usually a net charge on the family (now reinterpreted as a dynasty).

The effects of changes in the rates of interest on consumption are slightly more complicated here than in the case of no altruism because, at any date, the family can be a net borrower or a net lender. Therefore, a rise in r^t will still induce the family to substitute c_2^t for c_1^t, and c_3^{t-1} for c_2^{t-1}. But, if the family is a net lender at that date, there will be positive income effects which could cause a rise, or prevent a fall, of c_2^{t-1} and c_1^t.

The difference between the altruistic and the non-altruistic case is more fundamental where the effect of interest rates on fertility is concerned. Without altruism, the demand for the number of children is, in fact, derived from that for old-age consumption. Here, by contrast, the quantity of children is a good in its own right. If the physiological constraint is not binding, a rise in r^t will then have a substitution effect on t^t. As we can see from (9.43)–(9.44), the sign of this effect will be negative if y^{t+1} is large enough for the net cost of a child to rise with the rate of interest, positive otherwise. Additionally, there may be a positive or negative income effect, according to whether the family is in a net lending or borrowing position. If the other interest rates stay put as r^t rises, the income effect of this change is likely to be small relative to the substitution effect, because fertility at t will be substituted for or by fertility at other dates, as well as for or by parental consumption at t. That, however, does not eliminate the ambiguity of the overall effect of r^t on n^t, because the direction of these inter-generational substitutions is ambiguous anyway.

On the face of it, it thus seems that, where fertility decisions are concerned, an altruistic family responds to interest-rate changes in much the same way as a selfish one. All that seems to have changed, with the introduction of altruism, is that fertility is now less likely to rise with the market rate of interest. There is, however, a much more important, if obvious, difference: given altruism towards parents (as well as children), family solidarity is in no danger of breaking down if the market rate of interest rises too much, or if a capital market becomes accessible for the first time.

In conclusion, a couple that does not derive any direct

utility from quantity and quality of children will respond to the development of a sufficiently attractive alternative to the family transfer system by having no children at all, while one that does may respond by reducing its fertility, but not to zero. Neither couple will support its own parents unless it feels altruistic towards them. The phenomenon to which we referred at the end of Section 9.2, namely that fertility appears to fall drastically, but not to zero, with the development and widespread availability of market (or State) based methods of providing for old age may thus be taken as additional evidence that, for some couples at least, children are a source of direct utility. Whether they are or not, however, the demand for them will decrease as the old-age security motive for having children disappears. We have, therefore, another reason, in addition to the high level of wage rates generally and female wage rates in particular, why fertility rates are so low in mature economies. The phenomenon of the abandonment of old people by their grown-up children when the family transfer system ceases to be competitive with the alternative—also mentioned earlier in this chapter—is evidence, for its part, that altruism towards previous generations is not universal.

9.5. Bequests and Filial Attention

So far in this book we have only examined the possibility of transfers of time from one generation to the next, but not the other way round. In reality, however, we observe middle-aged people looking after older, as well as younger, relatives. This possibility can be easily allowed for in all the models considered in the present chapter by assuming that the good consumed by the old, c_3, is domestically produced by means of commodities, e, purchased from the market, and of time, a, supplied by the next generation (now middle-aged). Therefore, for any t,

$$c_3^t = F(e^t, a^t), \tag{9.45}$$

where $F(\ )$ is a domestic production function with the usual properties.

Since the time dedicated by the middle-aged to the care of the old could have otherwise been sold on the labour market, the total opportunity cost of the attention received, in old age, by each member of generation $(t-1)$ is clearly $a^{t-1}w^{t+1}$, where w^{t+1} is the market wage rate at the date when the transfer takes place. The difference between this opportunity cost, divided by the ratio between middle-aged and old family members at date $(t+1)$, and the amount of commodities, b^t, transferred by the old to the middle-aged at that same date gives us the net value of the transfer to generation $(t-1)$ made at date $(t+1)$ by each member of generation t,

$$d^t \equiv \frac{a^{t-1}w^{t+1}}{n^{t-1}} - b^t. \tag{9.46}$$

This replaces (9.34) and, note, applies irrespective of whether the family has access to a capital market or not.

Assuming altruism, as in the models of the last section, the allocation of each middle-aged family member's time between the labour market and the care of old relatives will be governed by the condition that, for $t = 2,3,4, \ldots$,

$$\frac{F_a^{t-2}}{F_e^{t-2}} = w^t, \tag{9.47}$$

where F_a^{t-2} and F_e^{t-2} denote the marginal product of, respectively, a^{t-2} and e^{t-2} in terms of c_3^{t-2}. Furthermore, the right-hand side of (9.41) will be multiplied by F_e^t.

Since (9.47) is an efficiency condition (it says that the marginal valuation, in terms of commodities, of time employed in the care of the old must be equated to its marginal opportunity cost), it would also hold in the absence of altruism if the rules governing the conduct of family members were designed to achieve a Pareto-optimum.[9] We may thus envisage a situation where the old would use part of the loan repayments made by the next generation to buy attention from their, now middle-aged, children at the market wage rate (or, equivalently, a situation where the repayment would be partly in commodities and partly in personal services).

It has been argued,[10] however, that selfish old people could extract a better deal from their grown-up children (i.e. pay less than the market rate) if, instead of paying for attention as they went along, they promised to pay for it all at once at the date of death. The idea is that each parent would irrevocably fix the total size of the estate early on, and write the testament (the terms of which would be disclosed to the potential beneficiaries) in such a way that the child who gave the parent most attention would get the lot or, if all children behaved equally well, everyone would get the same. The parent would thus be organizing, in effect, an auction in which the children are invited to bid against one another (there has to be more than one). If the bidders cannot collude, a skilful auctioneer (or, in our case, a skilfully drafted testament) can in such an auction extract from the successful bidder or bidders the full consumer surplus generated by the transaction. In other words, those who did inherit would be no better off than if they had paid no attention to the parent and got no bequest.

The attraction of this argument is that it provides a possible explanation of why people pass at least part of their wealth on to their children in the form of bequests, even though gifts *inter vivos* usually attract a lower rate of tax (and can more easily elude taxation altogether). The weakness in the argument is that it presupposes that the children cannot collude, while, in reality, they most certainly can. All they have to do, to counteract the parent's strategy, is agree among themselves that only one of them will pay any attention (and in minimal amount!) to the parent, so that only one child will inherit, and that the child who does inherit will then share with all the others. Any incentive to go back on the agreement would be removed by the children signing, before the parent's death, a perfectly legal document commiting them to redistribute any bequests among themselves so as to give each one the same share of the estate.[11]

It thus seems that, in the absence of filial altruism, parents could not get away with paying less than the market rate for their grown-up children's services. On the contrary, it may be argued that, since the children can sell their time on the labour market, while parents have no alternative to buying filial attention from their children, the latter could collectively exploit this asymmetry to charge the former more than the market rate. As well as extracting a premium over the market rate of interest from the young, the middle-aged would thus be extracting a premium over the market wage rate from the old. That being the case, the old would have nothing to gain from rewarding their children's attention with bequests rather than straight payments *inter vivos*.

How, then, can we explain bequests, without conceding irrationality, in situations where bequests are less tax-efficient than gifts *inter vivos*? In the absence of altruism (from and to children), bequests could arise from uncertainty about age of death. Risk-averse people would then save, in middle age, more than they expect to consume in old age, because they are afraid of being caught short if they live longer than expected. If that were the case, we should observe that the size of the estate *decreases* as the age of death of the testator increases, but there is some evidence that the opposite may be true.[12]

Altruism, by itself, does not make much difference to the point at issue. It explains why the old may wish to make transfers to the middle-aged in excess of the market value of the personal services supplied by the latter, but does not justify making the transfer in a form (bequest) that will attract higher taxes. Suppose, however, that adjoining generations do not share the same view of how family resources should be deployed. As pointed out in Section 9.3, that could happen in the case where parents are altruistic towards children but not the other way round even if every generation has the same preferences, i.e. the same function $U(\ )$, because those preferences might not be time-consistent. If, on the other hand, altruism between generations were mutual, as assumed in the last section, a divergence of views would imply a difference of preferences, i.e. that different generations have different $W(\ )$. Whichever is the case, if generation $(t + 1)$ will not do of its own accord what generation t wishes it to do, generation t will have a motive for delaying making any transfer to generation $(t + 1)$ as long as possible. Suppose, for example, that parents like to bring up young children in rather Spartan fashion (for the children's own good, of course, since we are assuming altruism), while the grandparents would have them thoroughly spoilt. The grandparents could then delay passing their wealth on to the children's parents to the last possible moment (and dangle the implicit threat of making bequests directly to the grandchildren) as a means of changing their children's behaviour.

Bequests may thus be explained by a combination of intergenerational altruism, which gives each generation a positive interest in the welfare of its successors, and of disagreement (due either to time-inconsistent preferences, or to straightforward differences of preferences) between generations, which may induce a generation to hang on to wealth as long as possible for the power it gives it over its successors.[13] This explanation is consistent with the evidence of very limited take-up of annuity schemes by retired people. Were it not for the power that wealth confers, it would in fact be rational for old people to want to swap any assets they may have for an annuity.[14] That would allow them to spend as much as possible (not only on themselves, but also on their children) in their lifetime, without the risk of being caught short if they live longer than expected, but would leave them with nothing to bequeath. The reason why so many people forgo this opportunity to maximize their lifetime spending power may be precisely that, for paternalistic rather than selfish reasons, they want to retain some leverage over their descendants' behaviour.

NOTES

1. The forward transfer, from middle to old age, could be accomplished even without a capital market if commodities (the stuff 'income' is made of) were storable. We shall assume, however, that this is not the case, i.e. that commodities not consumed vanish at the end of the current period.
2. That is certainly so, in reality, until the would-be borrower reaches the legal age of majority, and it remains so even later, to some extent, if the person in question does not have sufficient assets to offer as security.
3. That, notice, would also be true if the young could actually bargain (from birth) with their parents and other middle-aged relatives, but still could not borrow on the open market. The asymmetry between their respective positions would in fact give middle-aged lenders a bargaining advantage that would allow them to extract from young borrowers a premium over the commercial rate.
4. We assume, realistically, that the middle-aged cannot borrow from the market against the transfers that they expect to receive in old age through the family network. Otherwise, the middle-aged would want to 'lend' unlimited amounts to the young at the domestic interest rate and, at the same time, borrow from the market at the lower interest rate available there.
5. Provided that the physiological constraint (9.4) is not binding.
6. That has the distasteful implication that parents are indifferent between not having a child, and having a child who would die immediately after birth for lack of sustenance. This goes to show how extreme the assumption of total selfishness is.
7. In this and the next section we shall make no distinction between these two forms of transfer. Possible reasons for preferring one to the other will be examined in Sec. 9.5.
8. Becker and Barro (1988) analyse a particular form of time-consistent model under the *assumption* that transfers to children (interpreted as bequests) can be negative. They assume, in other words, that children are obliged to pick up any debts left behind by their parents. Barro and Becker (1989) re-examine the same model in a general equilibrium setting.
9. In that case, the right-hand side of (9.8) also would be multiplied by F_e^t.
10. See Bernheim *et al.* (1985).
11. Collusion among participants is possible in any kind of auction and, indeed, rigged auctions are not uncommon. In public auctions,

however, collusion is generally illegal and, furthermore, it might not be easy for each participant to find out how much the others have bid (e.g. because bids are sealed) until it is too late. By contrast, filial collusion would not be illegal in a disguised auction like that organized by our crafty parent and, furthermore, the children could easily monitor each other's behaviour.

12. See, for example, Mirer (1980).
13. Given this divergence of views, however, it would be more appropriate to describe the attitude of one generation towards the next as paternalistic, rather than altruistic.
14. The largest asset most people have is the house in which they live, but there are schemes whereby the house can be exchanged for a regular cash payment *plus* the use of the house for the rest of life.

10

Policy Issues

Throughout this book we have looked at the way families and individuals respond to their economic environment, an important part of which is the system of taxes and subsidies that the government of the day has chosen to implement. In this final chapter, we look at the considerations that may have led the government to that particular choice of policy instruments.[1]

Government intervention, in one form or another, can be justified on equity or efficiency grounds. Equity considerations arise from the fact that the utility function of the government is, in a democratic society, an aggregation of the utility functions of the governed. In particular, if government preferences are characterized by diminishing marginal rates of substitution of the utility of any one citizen or family for any other (in the same way as the preferences of any family or individual are supposed to be characterized by diminishing marginal rates of substitution of any good for any other), the maximization of the government's utility will lead to policies that transfer resources from the more to the less fortunate. These issues are examined in the earlier part of the present chapter.

Efficiency considerations arise from what, in contexts different from the present one, is called 'market failure': a situation where the interaction of individuals and groups of individuals (such as families and firms) does not generate a Pareto-optimal outcome. Such situations are associated with divergences of private costs or benefits from social costs or benefits. In the latter part of this chapter we examine ways in which government intervention may eliminate a source of inefficiency, but also ways in which the government itself can unwittingly cause inefficiency.

10.1. *Horizontal Redistribution*

We start by considering the case of a government interested in redistributing resources among families and, perhaps, in financing the provision of some given volume of public goods. We assume, for this purpose, that the government has no quarrel with the way each family allocates resources across generations—only that, for some reason, it would like to make some families a little happier than they would otherwise be and, perhaps, others a little less happy. The government will then want to set up a system of taxes and subsidies that, taking into account the families' responses to those taxes and subsidies, and subject to its own budgetary restrictions, will achieve the distribution of utility across families that it regards as the most desirable.[2]

As the focus is, at this stage, on inter-family rather than intergenerational issues, it seems appropriate to take the model set out in the first four sections of Chapter 7 as a description of family behaviour. The predictions of that model are, in any case, consistent with those of the explicitly intertemporal and intergenerational model discussed in Chapter 9. We shall assume, further, that market conditions are not affected by small variations in the tax-benefit system, so that, in particular, (gross) wage rates are invariant to income-tax changes. For simplicity, we shall restrict our attention to linear tax systems, made up of a lump-sum subsidy, so much per family, denoted by ψ, of a tax on earnings at the rate $(\theta_i - 1)$, which may be different for mother $(i = m)$ and father $(i = f)$, and of a tax on bequests at the rate[3] $(\tau - 1)$.

The net tax bill (which may, of course, be negative) of a family may be written as

$$t = (\theta_f - 1)F + (\theta_m - 1)M + (\tau - 1)B - \phi_n - \psi, \quad (10.1)$$

where

$$F \equiv w_f L_f, \tag{10.2}$$
$$M \equiv w_m L_m, \tag{10.3}$$

and

$$B \equiv bn \tag{10.4}$$

denote, respectively, the father's net earnings, the mother's net earnings, and the net bequests made by the parents in question. As in Chapter 7, w_i and L_i are, respectively, the net wage rate and the labour supply of parent i (i = f,m), while b is the net bequest made to each child and n the number of children. Tax rates are again expressed as fractions of the *net* sum (earnings, bequests) left over after paying the tax. The family's full income is defined by

$$Y \equiv w_f L_f + w_m L_m + \psi + B^0, \tag{10.5}$$

where B^0 denotes net bequests received by the parents in question.

Suppose that the government's own preferences are represented by the welfare function

$$V = \Sigma_j V_j(U_j), \tag{10.6}$$

where U_j stands for the utility of the jth family (with $j = 1,2, \ldots, N$, and N 'large'), as determined by (7.1), and the function $V_j(\ )$ is twice differentiable, non-decreasing, and concave. This representation of government preferences allows for a very wide range of preference structures. At one extreme, it allows for the possibility that the government may have extremely egalitarian preferences, in which case the marginal contribution to welfare of the utility of the jth family, $V_j'(U_j)$, will be equal to unity for the most disadvantaged family, the one with the lowest utility, and zero for everyone else. That is the Rawlsian case. Towards the opposite end of the political spectrum (10.6) allows also for the possibility that $V_j'(U_j)$ may equal the inverse of the marginal utility of income to family j. That may be called the *laissez-faire* case, because the government would then have no desire to change the relative distribution of utility across families. The only reason why the government might wish to intervene in such a case, is in order to finance the provision of some predetermined volume of public goods.[4] The classical Benthamite case, where the government's aim is to maximize the unweighted sum of the utilities of its citizens, i.e. where $W'_j(U_j)$ is equal to unity for all j, lies somewhere between the *laissez-faire* and the Rawlsian case.

The government budget constraint is given by

$$\Sigma_j t_j = R, \tag{10.7}$$

where t_j is the tax bill of the jth family, and R the required level of expenditure on public goods. The first-order conditions for the maximization of (10.6), subject to (10.7) and to family behaviour,[5] are

$$\sum_j \left[\frac{\partial t_j}{\partial \theta_f} - v_j F_j \right] = 0, \tag{10.8}$$

$$\sum_j \left[\frac{\partial t_j}{\partial \theta_m} - v_j M_j \right] = 0, \tag{10.9}$$

$$\sum_j \left[\frac{\partial t_j}{\partial \theta} + v_j n_j \right] = 0, \tag{10.10}$$

$$\sum_j \left[\frac{\partial t_j}{\partial \tau} - vj B_j \right] = 0, \tag{10.11}$$

and

$$\sum_j \left[\frac{\partial t_j}{\partial \psi} + v_j \right] = 0, \tag{10.12}$$

where F_j, M_j, B_j, and n_j denote, respectively, net paternal earnings, net maternal earnings, net bequests made (in total, not per child) and number of children raised in the jth family. The term

$$v_j \equiv V'_j(U_j)(\lambda_j/\mu), \tag{10.13}$$

where λ_j stands for the marginal utility of full income[6] to the jth family, and μ for the marginal welfare contribution of government revenue,[7] represents the government's marginal valuation, expressed in terms of public expenditure, of the *j*th family's full income. We shall refer to it as the welfare weight of family *j*. Each of the bracketed expressions in (10.8)–(10.12) thus represents the net benefit, in the government's eyes, of a marginal transfer to (in the case of a subsidy) or from (in the case of a tax) family *j*.

Taking the second term in each of these conditions to the right of the equality sign, and dividing each term of (10.8)–(10.11) by the corresponding term in (10.12), we find

$$-\frac{\Sigma_j(\partial t_j/\partial\theta_f)}{\Sigma_j(\partial t_j/\partial\psi)} = \frac{\Sigma_j v_j F_j}{\Sigma_j v_j} \equiv \tilde{F}, \tag{10.14}$$

$$-\frac{\Sigma_j(\partial t_j/\partial\theta_m)}{\Sigma_j(\partial t_j/\partial\psi)} = \frac{\Sigma_j v_j M_j}{\Sigma_j v_j} \equiv \tilde{M}, \tag{10.15}$$

$$\frac{\Sigma_j(\partial t_j/\partial\phi)}{\Sigma_j(\partial t_j/\partial\psi)} = \frac{\Sigma_j v_j n_j}{\Sigma_j v_j} \equiv \tilde{n}, \tag{10.16}$$

and

$$-\frac{\Sigma_j(\partial t_j/\partial\tau)}{\Sigma_j(\partial t_j/\partial\psi)} = \frac{\Sigma_j v_j B_j}{\Sigma_j v_j} \equiv \tilde{B}. \tag{10.17}$$

The term on the left of (10.14) is the amount by which the rate of tax on married men's earnings $(\theta_f - 1)$, must increase if the lump-sum subsidy, ψ, is raised a little, in order to keep the government budget in balance. Similarly, the term on the left of (10.15) is the amount by which the rate of tax on married women's earnings $(\theta_m - 1)$, must increase, while that on the left of (10.16) is the amount by which the child-benefit rate, ϕ, must decrease, and that on the left of (10.17) is the amount by which the rate of tax on bequests, $(\tau - 1)$, must increase, if ψ is raised a little. These left-hand-side expressions are, thus, marginal rates of financial substitution (MRFS): budgetary trade-offs showing how one policy instrument can be substituted for another, at the margin, taking into account the family behaviour described by the model of Chapter 7.

Conversely, the term on the right of (10.14) is the amount by which $(\theta_f - 1)$ must increase, if ψ is raised a little, in order to keep the government's utility, V, constant. Similarly, the terms on the right of (10.15) to (10.17) are the amounts by which the corresponding policy instruments must increase (in the case of a tax) or decrease (in the case of a subsidy) if ψ is raised a little. They are, therefore, policy trade-offs or marginal rates of welfare substitution (MRWS), reflecting the government's political inclination. These MRWS turn out to be averages, taken across families, of, respectively, paternal and maternal earnings, number of children raised, and net bequests made, weighted with the welfare weight of each family.

In general, the calculation of these policy trade-offs will require a detailed specification of the welfare function $V(\ )$ and of the underlying model of family behaviour. Not so, however, in the Rawlsian and in the *laissez-faire* case. In the former, $\tilde{F}$, $\tilde{M}$, $\tilde{B}$, and $\tilde{n}$ are, in fact, equal to, respectively, paternal earnings, maternal earnings, net bequests made, and number of children raised in the most disadvantaged family. In the latter, they are equal to the simple arithmetic mean of paternal earnings, maternal earnings, net bequests, and number of children across all families.

If we are now prepared to assume that no elected government would deliberately set out to make society *more* unequal than it would be without its intervention, and since one cannot be more egalitarian than Rawls, we may take the *laissez-faire* and the Rawlsian specifications of the welfare function as limiting cases within which all the others will fall. We can then conclude that the numerical value of $\tilde{F}$ will fall between the average level of paternal earnings and the level of paternal earnings in the most disadvantaged family.[8] Thus, if we do not know exactly what the government's preferences are, perhaps because the government itself is not capable of expressing them with sufficient precision, we can at least say that the tax-benefit system must be so designed that the MRFS between θ_f and ψ will fall between two easily estimatable figures: average paternal earnings and paternal earnings in the most disadvantaged family. Furthermore, we can say that the more egalitarian the government considers itself to be, the closer to the level of paternal earnings in the most disadvantaged family the MRFS in question has to get. By similar reasoning, we can also conclude that the other financial trade-offs must fall between the average level and the level in the most disadvantaged family—and closer to the latter, the more egalitarian the government is—of, respectively, maternal earnings, net bequests, and number of children.

10.2. *Tax Treatment of Married Couples*

As is generally the case in models of the kind we are examining here,[9] it is not easy to extract explicit fiscal rules from optimality conditions such as our (10.8)–(10.12). In order to come up with usable prescriptions one usually needs to know the functional form and numerical values of the parameters of the relationships that make up the model. Some policy indications can none the less be gleaned from the present model without going into specifics.

From (10.14) and (10.15) we deduce that, at a welfare maximum,

$$\frac{\theta_f}{\theta_m} = \frac{\xi_f \tilde{M}}{\xi_m \tilde{F}}, \tag{10.18}$$

where

$$\xi_i \equiv \frac{\theta_i}{t} \frac{\partial t}{\partial \theta_i} (i = f\ m) \tag{10.19}$$

is an elasticity, telling us by what percentage the net government revenue, $t \equiv \Sigma_j t_j$, will vary if θ_i is raised by one per cent. Given (10.1), we can also write

$$\xi_f = \frac{\theta_f F}{t} - \Sigma_j(\alpha_{Fj}\beta_j^{ff} + \alpha_{Mj}\beta_j^{fm} + \alpha_{Bj}\beta_j^{fB} - \alpha_{nj}\beta_j^{fn})$$

$$(10.20)$$

and

$$\xi_m = \frac{\theta_m M}{t} - \Sigma_j(\alpha_{Mj}\beta_j^{mm} + \alpha_{Fj}\beta_j^{mf} + \alpha_{Bj}\beta_j^{mB} - \alpha_{nj}\beta_j^{mn})$$

$$(10.21)$$

where $F \equiv \Sigma_j F_j$ and $M \equiv \Sigma_j M_j$ are the aggregate net earnings of married men and women, respectively. The symbols

$$\alpha_{Fj} \equiv \frac{(\theta_f - 1)F_j}{t}, \; \alpha_{Mj} \equiv \frac{(\theta_m - 1)M_j}{t},$$

$$\alpha_{Bj} \equiv \frac{(\tau - 1)B_j}{t} \text{ and } \alpha_{nj} \equiv \frac{\theta n_j}{t}$$

$$(10.22)$$

denote the shares in the net government revenue of the taxes paid or subsidies received by family j on, respectively, paternal earnings, maternal earnings, bequests made, and number of children raised. As for

$$\beta_j^{if} \equiv \frac{w_{ij}}{L_{fj}} \frac{\partial L_{fj}}{\partial w_i}, \; \beta_j^{im} \equiv \frac{w_{ij}}{L_{mj}} \frac{\partial L_{mj}}{\partial w_i}, \; \beta_j^{iB} \equiv \frac{w_{ij}}{B_j} \frac{\partial B_j}{\partial w_{ij}},$$

and $\beta_j^{in} \equiv \frac{w_{ij}}{n_j} \frac{n_j}{\partial w_{ij}},$

$$(10.23)$$

these are the elasticities of, respectively, the father's labour supply, the mother's labour supply, net bequests and number of children to the net wage rate of parent i in family j.

Equation (10.18) tells us that, other things being equal, (θ_m/θ_f) must increase with (ξ_m/ξ_f). Keeping in mind that one of the components (possibly the largest) of ξ_i is the negative of i's own-wage elasticity of labour[10] (10.18) is a generalization of the well-known rule that the rate of tax on earnings must vary inversely with the wage elasticity of the labour supply. Intuitively that rule can be explained by saying that, the less a source of government revenue shrinks when it is taxed, the easier it is for the government to get revenue from it. However, if there is more than one type of tax (on various categories of earners, or on different objects) and there are also subsidies of one kind or another, then the tax authority must take into account not only the direct effect of any tax rate on the yield of that particular tax, but also the indirect effects of that tax rate on the yield of other taxes and on the take-up of subsidies. That gives us the more general principle, embedded in (10.18), that the rate at which a tax is levied should increase in proportion to the elasticity of government revenue to that rate of tax. Can we infer from this whether married men's earnings should be taxed at a higher rate than married women's, or the other way round?

Let us start by comparing the right-hand sides of (10.20) and (10.21). In the light of the theoretical arguments and empirical evidence presented in Chapters 2 and 7, we expect the aggregate earnings of married men, F, to be larger than those of married women, M. For the same reason, we expect the own-wage elasticity of the labour supply of married women to be more positive, and the cross-wage elasticity to be less negative, than the corresponding elasticities of married men ($\beta_j^{mm} > \beta_j^{ff}$ and $\beta_j^{mf} > \beta_j^{fm}$). Furthermore, we expect fertility to respond negatively to the mother's net wage rate ($\beta_j^{mn} < 0$) and positively to the father's ($\beta_j^{fn} > 0$). All this points towards ξ_f being larger than ξ_m. On the other hand, net bequests are likely to respond more positively to the father's than to the mother's net wage rate ($\beta_j^{fB} > \beta_j^{mB}$) but that is unlikely to alter the relative size of ξ_f and ξ_m, because the share of estate duties in the government revenue ($\Sigma_j \alpha_{Bj}$) is typically very small.

Even assuming that ξ_f is larger than ξ_m, it does not necessarily follow, however, that θ_f should be larger than θ_m, because (ξ_f / ξ_m) is multiplied by ($\tilde{M}/\tilde{F}$). If the welfare function is *laissez-faire*, ($\tilde{M}/\tilde{F}$) will be equal to (M/F), in which case (10.18) tells us, quite simply, that the relative share of θ_i in the government revenue must be equated to its elasticity, ξ_i. For F sufficiently larger than M, it could then be optimal to tax married women's earnings at a *higher* rate than married men's. But, suppose that, for some reason, $(\tilde{M}/\tilde{F})$ is higher, for any given (M/F), the closer the welfare function is to the Rawlsian specification. Then, the more egalitarian the government preferences are, the more likely it is that married women's earnings should be taxed at a *lower* rate than married men's. We come back to this point in the next section.

10.3. *The Implications of Egalitarianism*

The characteristics of an optimal choice[11] of the policy instruments ψ, θ_i, ϕ, and τ are illustrated in Fig. 10.1. The continuous curve in panel (*a*) is an isorevenue curve, showing combinations of θ_f and ψ that, given the choice of the other policy instruments, and given the way families respond to different policy packages, will satisfy the government budget constraint (i.e. equate the government's net revenue to R). This curve is upward-sloping because a rise in the rate of tax on married men's earnings $(\theta_f - 1)$ would make it possible to pay each family a higher lump-sum subsidy ψ. The concavity of the curve indicates that the rise in ψ made possible by a rise in θ_f gets smaller and smaller as θ_f increases. This reflects an assumption—justified by everything we found in Chapters 2 and 7—that the aggregate labour supply of married men will fall, as θ_f rises, because families will substitute paternal by maternal earnings as sources of income, and market commodities by home-time as inputs into the domestic production of goods.

Panels (*b*), (*c*), and (*d*) of Fig. 10.1 can be similarly interpreted. In (*b*) and (*d*), the isorevenue curve is upward-sloping and concave to indicate that ψ can be raised by smaller and smaller amounts, as the tax rate $(\theta_m - 1)$ or $(\tau - 1)$ is raised, because the tax base (married women's

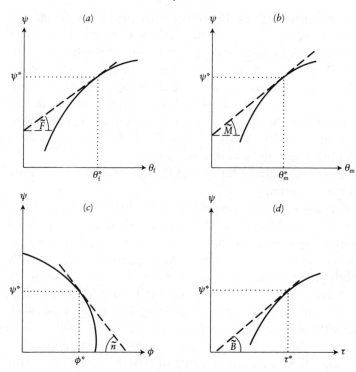

Fig. 10.1

earnings or bequests) will get smaller. In panel (c), the isorevenue curve is downward sloping and concave to the origin to indicate that ψ must be reduced by larger and larger amounts, as the rate of subsidy payable for each child (ϕ) is raised, because families will have more children.

The absolute slopes of the isorevenue curves portrayed in panels (a), (b), (c), and (d) of Fig. 10.1 are the MRFS of, respectively, θ_f, θ_m, ϕ, and τ for ψ. At the optimal point $(\psi^*, \theta_f^*, \theta_m^*, \phi^*, \tau^*)$, the MRFS of θ_f are equal to $\tilde{F}$, those of θ_m to $\tilde{M}$, etc. as prescribed by (10.14)–(10.17). Let us now suppose that the specification of the welfare function which generated $(\psi^*, \theta_f^*, \theta_m^*, \phi^*, \tau^*)$ is somewhere between the *laissez-faire* and the Rawlsian extremes. How would the policy recipe change if the specification of the welfare function changed a little, e.g. if it shifted slightly towards the Rawlsian end of the spectrum?[12] In other words, if the government became a little more egalitarian, would it become optimal to tax and subsidize families more, or less, and in what form? Since the change of government preferences would raise the welfare weights of the less-advantaged families, we need to know, in the first place, how the behaviour of those families differs from that of the more fortunate ones.

Let us start by considering a hypothetical case where families are differentiated by the father's wage rate (earning ability) only. However unrealistic—because it implies, among other things, that all married women have the same earning ability, and that all couples have the same amount of inherited wealth—this assumption is actually one that is commonly made in optimal taxation models. Suppose, also, that the physiological ceiling on fertility is not binding on any of the families. The utility ranking of families then reflects their ranking in terms of paternal wage rates: the most disadvantaged family will be the one where the father has the lowest wage rate. In the light of earlier discussion, lower U_j will then be associated with lower F_j, higher M_j,[13] lower n_j, and, very likely, lower B_j.[14] Therefore, as the government becomes more egalitarian, $\tilde{B}$ will fall, $\tilde{M}$ will rise, $\tilde{n}$ will fall, and, probably, so will $\tilde{B}$.

Let us see what this implies for the choice of policy instruments. We can see from panel (*a*) of Fig. 10.1 that, if θ_m, ϕ, and τ were fixed at the levels θ_m^*, ϕ^*, and τ^*, the optimal value of θ_f would rise. Under similar circumstances, as we can see from the other three panels, the optimal θ_m and ϕ would fall, while the optimal τ would rise. This argument does not guarantee that the direction of the changes will be the one indicated if all the policy variables can be changed simultaneously,[15] because in that case the isorevenue curves may shift. It tells us, however, the direction of the substitution: greater egalitarianism will lead the government to substitute taxes on married men's earnings and on bequests for taxes on married women's earnings, and also to substitute lump-sum subsidies (independent of number of children) for subsidies related to number of children. This is intuitively appealing, because the families that the government wants to favour are those that have lower paternal earnings, raise fewer children, and make smaller bequests. It is in this case that, if the government is sufficiently egalitarian, it is optimal to tax married men's earnings at a higher rate than married women's (see last section).

Next, consider the symmetrically opposite case where the only difference between families is in the mother's wage rate (and continue to assume that the physiological constraint is not binding). In this case, $\tilde{F}$ will rise, $\tilde{M}$ will fall, $\tilde{n}$ will rise, and $\tilde{B}$ will also probably rise, as the government becomes more egalitarian. Therefore, following the same reasoning as before, the more egalitarian government will substitute taxes on married women's earnings for taxes on married men's earnings and taxes on bequests, and will also substitute child benefits for lump-sum subsidies. This is, again, as one would expect, because the government wants to help families where maternal earnings are lower, children more numerous, and the bequests made larger.

Another possibility is that families only differ in the amount of inherited wealth (and the physiological constraint on the number of children is still not binding). Here, $\tilde{F}$ and $\tilde{M}$ rise, while $\tilde{n}$ and $\tilde{B}$ fall, as the government becomes more egalitarian. In this case, it will be optimal to substitute taxes on bequests for taxes on the earnings of both parents, and lump-sum subsidies for child benefits. This, too, accords with intuition since the families upon which the government now looks more benignly have higher earnings (they work more, partly, because they have less property income), raise fewer children, and make smaller bequests.

Finally, let us look at the case where families only differ in their capacity to have children. If the physiological ceiling on fertility were not binding on anybody, families would then be effectively identical. Let us assume, however, that this constraint is binding on at least some of the families (obviously those with lower ceiling) so that lower utility is now associated with lower natural fecundity. In this case, as the government becomes more egalitarian, $\tilde{F}$ and $\tilde{M}$ will rise, $\tilde{n}$ will fall, and $\tilde{B}$ may go either way.[16] The more egalitarian government will then tend to reduce the tax rates on both categories of earnings, as those taxes are paid primarily by the more disadvantaged families, and also to reduce the rate of child benefits, as those go primarily to the luckier ones who can have more children. The optimal rate of tax on bequests could go up or down.

Matters become more complicated if families are differentiated by more than one characteristic, for example by paternal *and* maternal earning ability. Even in the simplest case, where the wage rates of husband and wife are positively correlated,[17] we cannot predict the effects of greater egalitarianism without numerical estimates of the elasticities of response of family behaviour to the various policy instruments, and of the means, variances, and covariance of married men's and married women's wage rates.[18]

In general, the direction of the optimal policy change, as government preferences change, will depend on the joint distribution of family characteristics (husband's and wife's earning abilities, inherited wealth, reproductive capacity, and, possibly, other traits not considered here). There seems to be no alternative, therefore, to calculating numerically, case by case, an optimal package of policy measures. None the less, the tentative conclusions reached on the basis of differences in one family characteristic at a time may have served to throw doubt on some commonly held views (invariably based on the analysis of models without endogenous fertility) about the direction of egalitarian policies.

For example, it is held by many that child benefits are a valuable instrument for channelling help towards the more disadvantaged sections of society. However, if child-bearing is, at least in the majority of cases, a voluntary activity, and parents do, on the whole, derive utility from the quantity and quality of their children, then it is not obvious that couples with more children should necessarily attract the benevolence of the egalitarian policy-maker. Indeed, if the ability to reproduce were the only distinguishing feature, the more disadvantaged families would be the ones with less, not with more, children. And, even in the other cases considered, greater egalitarianism was not always found to imply higher child benefits: it was so in the case where deprivation arose from low maternal wage rate, but not where it derived from low paternal wage rate, or from low inherited wealth.

Similar observations can be made about taxation. Leaving aside the enforceability question, a tax on bequests is generally regarded as 'egalitarian'. We found, however, that greater egalitarianism may involve a lower rate of tax on bequests if lower family utility is associated with lower maternal wage rate. With regard to the taxation of earnings, also, it does not seem justified to presume that greater egalitarianism necessarily implies higher tax rates, or the more severe fiscal treatment of one marriage partner relative to the other. Where low utility was associated with low inherited wealth or with lower capacity to have children, our analysis indeed pointed to lower tax rates on the earnings of both partners. The direction of the change in the relative tax rate was clear only in the cases where the utility ranking of families reflected either paternal or maternal wage rate ranking alone.

10.4. *A Public Pension System*

Another possible reason for wanting to interfere with individual and family choices may be that the government disagrees with the way families and markets allocate resources over the life-cycle and across generations. The most wide-spread, and most intrusive, form of government intervention in this sphere is the creation of a public pension scheme, that collects compulsory contributions (a tax, for all practical intents and purposes) from citizens of working age, and makes payments to citizens of pensionable age. Indeed, the tax-benefit system as a whole may be regarded as a means of altering the life cycle and intergenerational allocation of resources because, among other things, it redistributes income from those of working age to the young and the old.

The sources of this possible disagreement may be several. It may be that the government paternalistically believes that individuals and families are not fully rational—i.e. that they discount the utility of future consumption and, as a result, make inadequate provisions for old age.[19] It may also be that the government is more egalitarian than families, and wishes to redistribute consumption from richer to poorer generations. Or, it could be that, for the reasons discussed in Sections 2 and 3 of the last chapter (a large and unexpected rise in the market rate of interest, or the unexpected opening of a capital market offering a high rate of interest), the family transfer system has broken down, and that the government has thus felt obliged to intervene in order to save the old from penury or even starvation.

The first two forms of disagreement imply that the government's objective function is different from those of families or individuals. The third, by contrast, presupposes something akin to 'market failure', a situation where the outcome of the unregulated interaction of individuals and private organizations is not Pareto-optimal. Notice that we are leaving aside the case, examined in the last three sections, where the government is interested in redistributing resources horizontally, across dynasties, rather than vertically, across generations of the same dynasty—even though some of the policy instruments (taxes on earnings and bequests, child benefits) used to achieve the former may incidentally result in the latter. Indeed, we shall abstract from questions of horizontal distribution by conducting the analysis that follows in terms of a representative dynasty.

Given that, for whatever reason, the government has decided to set up a public pension system, there is also the question of the form such a system should take. It could be 'fully funded', i.e. organized in such a way that the contributions levied on citizens of working age are invested at the best available interest rate, and that pensions are then paid from the proceeds of those investments. Alternatively, the system could be of the 'pay-as-you-go' variety, where pensions are paid out of current contributions.

Unlike a fully-funded system, pay-as-you-go has the disadvantage of being vulnerable to fluctuations of national income because, as already mentioned in Chapter 8, a reduction in the number of people of working age, or in their per-capita income, reduces the amount that can be paid out to current pensioners (unless the current workers are taxed more heavily, or other items of public expenditure are sacrificed). On the other hand, pay-as-you-go systems have the demagogic attraction that, at their inception, they can be used to pay generous pensions to generations who contributed little or nothing to their funding. Perhaps for this reason, public pension systems around the world are all essentially pay-as-you-go (i.e. have a very low ratio of reserves to commitments). As the system matures, however, each successive generation reaching pensionable age will have spent an increasing proportion of its working life contributing to the system. Therefore, higher and higher pensions would have to be paid to successive generations in order to offer them the same rate of return on their contributions as earlier generations.

Rises in the levels of the pensions are possible, in a pay-as-you-go system, if national income is growing sufficiently fast, and would amount to a systematic redistribution of resources from later to earlier generations (not necessarily from richer to poorer, because it may be numbers, rather than per-capita incomes, that are growing). If the pace of growth slackens, however, something has to give: either the level of the pension has to fall, or the level of the contribution has to rise, as a proportion of the contributor's income.[20] Either way, the rate of return on participating in the system will decrease, causing resentment, and will ultimately become unacceptable if it falls too far below the market rate of interest.

The experience of public pension systems in Western Europe, North America, and Japan bears this out. These systems started or reached their maximum extension in terms of quota of the population involved during the boom years of the 1960s. They entered a phase of continual financial crisis[21] in the 1970s with the world-wide recession triggered by the oil shocks of those years. The crisis continued, despite the economic upturn, in the 1980s, because of the falling ratio of people of working age to pensioners associated with declining fertility (low completed fertility and low tempo) and rising life expectancy. In the last three chapters, we have examined reasons why families have tended to substitute quantity of children with quality (of which life-expectancy is a manifestation). We shall argue, in what follows, that the presence of a pay-as-you-go pension system is an additional reason why couples want fewer children[22] and, therefore, that public pension systems as currently structured carry the seeds of their own distruction. The analytical framework is that of the last chapter.

10.5. *Vertical Redistribution*

Assume, for now, that individuals are selfish as in the first two sections of Chapter 9. Suppose that a pay-as-you-go public pension system is introduced, at date $(t + 1)$, such that every citizen born at t must pay what amounts to a tax (a compulsory contribution to the public pension fund) at $(t + 1)$, and will receive a pension at $(t + 2)$. Why should the government want to do that?

A reason could be, as already pointed out, that the family transfer system collapsed at t because it could no longer compete with the capital market. In that case, whatever the public sector has to offer would be better than nothing, because the present old, who had been counting on the support of the family network, would otherwise starve. Another reason could be that the family transfer system was still functioning at t, but the government decided—again for reasons that we have already discussed—that such a system did not make adequate provision for the old. Either way, the pension promised to each member of generation t by the public pension system will be at least as high as the transfer $\bar{d}^{t+1}\, \bar{n}^t$ that such a person would have received in old age through the extended family system (see Chapter 9).

If it has not collapsed already, the family transfer system will then collapse as a result of the introduction of a public pension system. Since the present middle-aged, at date $(t + 1)$, have no choice but to pay the tax, and are promised a pension at $(t + 2)$ independently of whether or not they support their elders and have children, they will then refuse to support the present old, and will have no children.[23] That way, they will be able to consume their whole disposable income (income minus the tax) at $(t + 1)$ in the expectation of being able to consume the promised pension at $(t + 2)$. That expectation will not be fulfilled, however, because there will not be a generation $(t + 1)$ and, therefore, there will be no middle-aged people at $(t + 2)$ to pay for their pensions.[24]

The sharpness of this conclusion reflects the crudity of the assumption of total lack of altruism. It serves, however, to highlight an externality associated with the presence of a pay-as-you-go pension system. While the system's ability to pay out old-age pensions to any generation increases with the number of children raised by that generation, the benefit to any couple from having a child is too small to be taken into account in fertility decisions, because the contribution to the pension fund that the child would make in future would not serve to pay the pensions of just that child's parents, but would be shared among all members of the parents' generation.

The incentive to have children could be restored by making pension entitlements increase with the number of children raised.[25] That, however, would raise questions of horizontal equity, because some couples will be more fecund than others.[26] More relevantly for our present pre-occupations, it would also have, on its own, adverse inter-temporal efficiency implications. If pension entitlements only depended on number of children, parents would in fact spend as little as possible for each child. Consumption in the first period of each generation's life would then be at subsistence level, which is unlikely to be Pareto-optimal.

In order to be efficient, i.e. to give rise to a Pareto-optimal allocation of resources across generations and over the life-cycle of each generation, a system of intergenerational transfers must satisfy, it will be recalled, (9.2)–(9.4) and (9.9). That is true whether the transfer system is administered by the extended family or by a public body. If it wishes to replace the family in this allocative role, the government must then take over that role entirely. It must, that is, prescribe how much the middle-aged have to pay not only to the old, but also to the young. There, however, the government is at a comparative disadvantage, because the amounts of time and commodities that parents dedicate to their young within the privacy of their homes are more difficult and costly to monitor by a public body than by the family itself.

Monitoring difficulties apart, how is the government to pick its policy package out of all those that are inter-temporally efficient? This brings us to the question of what the government's objective function might be. In a democratic context, one is used to thinking of government preferences being an aggregation of those of the governed.[27] As the governed do not care about the well-being of future genera-tions, we might then infer that the government would seek to maximize some weighted average of the utilities of its electors (the present old and the present middle-aged). However, the achievement of that maximum would require the implementation of the present government's policies by the next government that, having a different constituency, may wish to do otherwise. In other words, the next government might not treat its old (the present middle-aged) in the way the present government would wish it to, because it will have its middle-aged (the present young, about whom the present government does not care) to consider.

It is possible to get round this difficulty if per-capita income is constant over time, for in that special case the economy is capable of steady growth with constant n^t, c_i^t and, therefore, U^t for ever.[28] Conscious of its dependence on the decisions of subsequent governments for the realization of its policies, each government might then make it its objective to achieve the highest sustainable level of utility per head. Let us see what this implies, first, under the assumption of no capital market. Maximizing the utility function in (9.1), subject to (9.2)–(9.3)–(9.4)[29] for $c_i^t = c_i$, $d^t = d$, and $n^t = n$, yields

$$\frac{U_1}{U_2} = \frac{U_2}{U_3} = \frac{d}{c_1} = n. \qquad (10.24)$$

Let (c_i^*, d^*, n^*) be a solution to this problem. We shall then have that (d^*/c_1^*) equals n^*. If, at t, the government of the day prescribes $c_1^t = c_1^*$ and $d^t = d^*$, the middle-aged, who also face the constraints (9.2)–(9.3)–(9.4), will then choose $c_2^{t-1} = c_2^*$, $c_3^{t-1} = c_3^*$, and $n^{t-1} = n^*$. The same will be true for every t.[30]

If there is a capital market, and assuming that the market rate of interest is constant, $r^t = r$, the maximization of the sustainable level of utility will require

$$n = r \qquad (10.25)$$

in addition to (10.24). Since individuals also will want to equate (U_2/U_3) to r, the conclusions reached for the case without a capital market still stand. Furthermore, it makes no difference whether the public pension system is pay-as-you-go or fully funded, because the revenue from the investment of the taxes paid by each generation will be equal to the taxes paid by the subsequent generation.

All that was under the assumption of no altruism between generations. In the presence of altruism, there may still be scope for government intervention if, as assumed in Section 9.3, individuals are altruistic towards their children, but not towards their parents. Even though people love their children, the per-capita income of a generation may, in fact, be sufficiently low, by comparison with those of subsequent generations, for its members to want greater old-age support than the extended family system will provide.[31] In that case, a government maximizing a weighted average of the utility functions of the present old and middle-aged would set out to modify the intertemporal allocation brought about by the family.

Such a situation would not arise, however, if people were altruistic towards their parents, as well as towards their children, as assumed in Section 9.4. In those circumstances, the reason for government intervention in this sphere could only be paternalism: the belief, possibly well founded,[32] that a sufficiently large number of families is not capable (while some public body is) of carrying out the complex reasoning and calculations necessary to work out an optimal life cycle and intergenerational allocation.

10.6. *Concluding Remarks*

The arguments treated in the present chapter far from exhaust the list of situations in which government intervention would be beneficial or justifiable. Externalities and co-ordination failures can arise in a wide variety of situations other than those examined here.[33] In particular, unregulated individual or family choices could be inefficient in the face of decreasing or increasing returns to scale (the former associated with the presence of fixed or exhaustible natural resources, the latter with the presence of some forms of technical progress)[34] for the economy as a whole. Such issues are more properly dealt with in a population-economics context, where markets and families are allowed to interact,[35] than in a book which looks in detail at the workings of families and other households, taking market conditions as given.

The biggest lacuna, however, is the absence of any discussion of basic forms of public intervention such as the provision of sanitation, medical, and educational facilities. In less developed countries, particularly in the very poorest, where it cannot be taken for granted that families already have access to those facilities either through the State or through the market, public provision is known to have very large effects on quantity and quality of children. But any less than superficial attempt at dealing with that would have taken us deep into development-economics territory. The policy issues examined here have been those that could be linked most naturally with the subject-matter of earlier chapters.

NOTES

1. For a review, against a household-economics background, of the welfare-theoretic concepts and terminology used in this chapter, see the first three chapters of Nerlove *et al.* (1987).
2. The analysis that follows draws on Cigno (1986).
3. If we wish to allow for the fact that transfers to children in the form of bequests take place *later* than transfers in other forms, we may think of τ as the ratio between a tax factor and an interest factor. See Chap. 9 for a full examination of the time-structure of the problem.
4. We are implicitly saying, therefore, that (10.6) may be a sub-welfare function, and that the volume of public goods to be supplied may have been determined by maximizing the full welfare function.
5. This implies that the solution to this optimization problem will be a *second best*, i.e. it will be the best that the government can achieve,

given that it can only affect resource allocation indirectly, by influencing the behaviour of families and individuals with taxes and subsidies. A *first-best* solution would require that the government could maximize the welfare function subject only to resource constraints (i.e. if it could directly dispose of national resources as in a centrally planned economy).

6. The Lagrange multiplier associated with the family budget constraint (7.2) encountered in Chap. 7.

7. The Lagrange multiplier associated with the family budget constraint (10.7).

8. Most disadvantaged does not necessarily mean poorest, because the maximized utility of a family depends on its child-rearing technology (or, more generally, on its home-production technology), as well as on its inherited wealth and earning capacity. Given a common technology, however, the most disadvantaged family would be the poorest.

9. The prototypes are Mirrlees (1971, 1972).

10. More precisely, one of the components of ξ_f is the negative of a weighted average of the own-wage elasticities of labour of married men. Similarly for ξ_m.

11. Which may not be unique.

12. This is a difficult question to answer in general terms, because we are talking of changing the parameters of the government objective function, rather than the parameters of one of the constraints as in the more usual comparative-statics exercises. Questions of this kind are usually dealt with by simulating a fully specified and estimated model for different numerical values of a parameter of the objective function.

13. Keep in mind that, as the mother's wage rate is the same in all families, its ratio to the father's wage rate will be higher in more disadvantaged families.

14. Recall that child quality is likely to be lower in families with lower w_f (see Chap. 7) and that, in those families, paternal time will substitute for income transfers, including bequests, to children in the production of quality. Hence, bequests per child, as well as number of children, are likely to be lower.

15. Indeed, our partial equilibrium approach leads us to conclude that ψ has to increase if the only other policy instrument varying is θ_f, ϕ, or τ, but that it has to decrease if the other variable instrument is θ_m.

16. Lower-utility families are likely to have larger earnings (because there are fewer children to look after) and, therefore, to make larger bequests per child, but have fewer children to make bequests to.

17. This leads to *assortative mating*. If the correlation were perfect, we

would then be in the situation considered in Chap. 1, where members of each sex unanimously rank members of the opposite sex according to one characteristic (earning ability in the present instance) only. In such a situation, as it will be recalled, the most desirable (highest-earning) man will marry the most desirable (highest-earning) woman, etc.

18. Boskin and Sheshinski (1983) estimate, for the USA, that the rate of tax on married women should be lower (about one-half) than that of married men, irrespectively of the degree of egalitarianism implicit in the government's objective function. This very strong result is based on data that show positive correlation between husband's and wife's wage rates, and compensated own-wage elasticity of labour supply much larger for married women than for married men. Although the government objective function used in that study is equivalent to our (10.6), however, labour supplies are determined by a conventional model of income–leisure choice (without endogenous fertility, etc.), and the policy instruments are accordingly restricted to the tax rates on husband's and wife's earnings, and a lump-sum subsidy (income guarantee).

19. See Diamond (1977) for an authoritative analysis of this and some of the other points discussed below.

20. Another possibility is to raise pensionable age, which does both things at the same time. Nothing of substance changes, on the other hand, if the pension fund is subsidized out of general taxation because, there too, either some tax rates will have to be raised or some benefit curtailed.

21. In the USA, for example, the reserves of the public pension system, that were still sufficient to pay out pensions for 12 months in 1970, were only sufficient for 6 months in 1977, and 1 month only in 1983. In West Germany, reserves had similarly fallen from 9 to 1.5 months between 1974 and 1980. See Cigno (1990*b*).

22. For a fuller discussion of the connection between pensions systems and fertility, see Cigno (1990*b*).

23. That, notice, is true irrespectively of whether individuals have access to the capital market or not because, even if they do, the domestic rate of interest will be higher than the market rate (see last chapter). If they do, however, the present middle-aged may be able to borrow against their future pensions that, unlike transfers expected to arrive through the family network, are guaranteed by the authority of the State and thus considered safe (see also n. 4 of the last chapter). In that case, it would not be possible for the government to enforce a shift of consumption from middle to old age larger than the one that individuals want.

24. This solvency problem would not arise (though there would still not be another generation after the present one) with a fully-funded pension system if the value of the assets held by the pension fund were independent of the size of the next generation, e.g. if the revenue from the social-security tax has been invested entirely abroad. However, that could not always be true. In an isolated economy, to take an extreme case, the assets collectively held by the old through the pension fund would become worthless if there were nobody of working age to man the real capital that stands behind those assets, and nobody to sell those assets to.

25. That is suggested in Bental (1989).

26. If the fertility ceiling is binding on the less fecund couples, equity considerations point towards a more, not less, favourable fiscal treatment of those couples; see Sec. 10.3.

27. That is, for example, the case of (10.6).

28. The constant per-capita income case is a little less special and, therefore, more interesting than it appears at first sight. Bental (1989) shows that, if real income is determined by a conventional aggregate production function with constant returns to scale and no technical progress, the pursuance of policies that maximize the steady-state level of utility per person would lead the economy to a steady state with constant per-capita income in one generation.

29. Notice that (9.3) is the budget constraint of a pay-as-you-go pension system, as well as the resource constraint of the old.

30. It would thus seem that, provided it can enforce c_i^*, the government can achieve a 'first-best' solution. In a sense, however, this also is a second-best solution, like the solution to the government optimization problem in Sec. 10.1, because we have justified the choice of this particular course of action by the present government with the need to take into account the behaviour of subsequent governments.

31. If individuals have access to the capital market, that support will be zero or negative; see Sec. 9.3.

32. See, again, Diamond (1977).

33. For a wider selection, see Nerlove *et al.* (1987).

34. See, for example, Cigno (1979, 1983*b*), Pitchford (1985).

35. See, for example, Pitchford (1974), Cigno (1981, 1984, 1988*a*).

Conclusion

This was an economist's book. Its primary aim was not to tell a story or make forecasts, but to establish functional relationships. None the less, some kind of story appears to have emerged from the theoretical argumentation and empirical evidence. As societies develop and mature, the optimal household size tends to become smaller and, at the same time, the role of the family as an allocator of resources and an organizer of transactions between generations tends to decline. Neither of these developments is caused, according to our analysis, by changes in preferences or culture. They are, rather, a response to changes in the structure of incentives and disincentives associated with the process of economic development. Indeed, some of what goes under the name of 'culture' in this as in other contexts may be interpreted as the debris of past states of the economic environment—a consequence of the fact that, when the structure of incentives and disincentives changes, it takes time to realize it, time to decide how best to respond to it, and time to modify the pattern of one's life.

What tends to be left of the role of families, in mature economies, is the provision of those goods for which neither the market nor the State can offer an acceptable substitute. In particular, the family remains—in one form or other—the institution where children are raised. But, as changes in relative prices make children more costly, and the development of alternative ways of providing for old age makes the benefit of having children smaller, the desire to have children and, with it, the importance of the family institution diminish.

The diminished importance of the family in mature economies does not make the study of the economics of the family any less important. For a start, most of the world is still a long way away from economic maturity. Second, that small part of the world that has reached maturity is beset, as we have seen, with the problem of an ageing population—a direct consequence of the low demand for quantity and high demand for quality of children that is characteristic of mature economies. And finally, the transition from the status of less developed to that of developed economy can bring with it severe problems of abandonment of the old, as the middle-aged discover that there are better ways of providing for one's own old age than submitting to family discipline. At all stages of economic development, therefore, it is important to understand how families, market, and State interact with one another. Indeed, the apparent inability of governments to anticipate and deal effectively with the problems mentioned may be fairly attributed to the insufficient attention so far given to those interactions.

References

BARMBY, T., and CIGNO, A. (1990), 'A Sequential Probability Model of Fertility Patterns', *Journal of Population Economics*, 3.

BARRO, R. J., and BECKER, G. S. (1989), 'Fertility Choice in a Model of Economic Growth', *Econometrica*, 57.

BECKER, G. S. (1960), 'An Economic Analysis of Fertility', in National Bureau of Economic Research, *Demographic and Economic Change in Developed Countries*, Princeton University Press, Princeton.

—— (1965), 'A Theory of the Allocation of Time', *Economic Journal*, 75.

—— (1973), 'A Theory of Marriage: Part I', *Journal of Political Economy*, 81.

—— (1974), 'A Theory of Marriage: Part II', *Journal of Political Economy*, 82.

—— (1981), *A Treatise on the Family*, Harvard University Press, Cambridge, Mass.

—— (1985), 'Human Capital, Effort and the Sexual Division of Labor', *Journal of Labor Economics*, 3.

—— and BARRO, R. J. (1988), 'A Reformulation of the Economic Theory of Fertility', *Quarterly Journal of Economics*, 103.

—— LANDES, E. M., and MICHAEL, R. T. (1977), 'An Economic Analysis of Marital Instability', *Journal of Political Economy*, 88.

—— and LEWIS, H. G. (1973), 'On the Interaction between the Quantity and Quality of Children', *Journal of Political Economy*, 81.

BEHRMAN, J. R., POLLAK, R. A., and TAUBMAN, P. (1982), 'Parental Preferences and Provision for Progeny', *Journal of Political Economy*, 90.

BEN-PORATH, Y. (1980), 'The F-connection: Families, Friends and Firms, and the Organization of Exchange', *Population and Development Review*, 6.

BENTAL, B. (1989), 'The Old Age Security Hypothesis and Optimal Population Growth', *Journal of Population Economics*, 1.

BERNHEIM, B. D., SHLEIFER, A., and SUMMERS, L. H. (1985), 'The Strategic Bequest Motive', *Journal of Political Economy*, 93.

BLINDER, A. S. (1973), 'A Model of Inherited Wealth', *Quarterly Journal of Economics*, 87.

—— (1976), 'Intergenerational Transfers and Life Cycle Consumption', *American Economic Review*, 66.

BLUNDELL, R., and WALKER, I. (1982), 'Modelling the Joint Determination of Household Labour Supplies and Commodities Demands' *Economic Journal*, 92.

BORENSTEIN, S., and COURANT, P. N. (1987), 'How to Carve a Medical Degree: Human Capital Assets in Divorce Settlements', Institute of Public Policy Studies Discussion Paper No. 269, University of Michigan.

BORSCH-SUPAN, A. (1986), 'Household Formation, Housing Prices and Public Policy Imports', *Journal of Public Economics*, 30.

BOSKIN, M. J., and SHESHINSKI, E. (1983), 'Optimal Tax Treatment of the Family: Married Couples', *Journal of Public Economics*, 20.

BOULIER, B. L., and ROSENZWEIG, M. R. (1984), 'Schooling, Search and Spouse Selection: Testing Economic Theories of Marriage and Household Behaviour', *Journal of Political Economy*, 92.

BUTZ, W. P., and WARD, M. P. (1979), 'The Emergence of Countercyclical US Fertility', *American Economic Review*, 69.

CAIN, G., and WATTS, H. (1973), *Labor Supply and Income Maintenance*, Academic Press, New York.

CALDWELL, J. C. (1978), 'A Theory of Fertility: From High Plateau to Destabilisation', *Population and Development Review*, 4.

CALHOUN, C. T., and ESPENSHADE, T. J. (1988), 'Childbearing and Wives' Foregone Earnings', *Populations Studies*, 42.

CIGNO, A. (1971), 'Economies of Scale and Industrial Location', *Regional Studies*, 5.

—— (1979), 'Depletion of Natural Resources and Accumulation of Capital when Population is Endogenous', *Metroeconomica*, 1.

—— (1981), 'Growth with Exhaustible Resources and Endogenous Population', *Review of Economic Studies*, 48.

—— (1983*a*), 'On Optimal Family Allowances', *Oxford Economic Papers*, 35.

—— (1983*b*), 'Human Capital and the Time-Profile of Human Fertility', *Economics Letters*, 13.

—— (1984), 'Consumption vs. Procreation in Economic Growth', in G. Steinmann (ed.), *Economic Consequences of Population Change in Industrialised Countries*, Springer-Verlag, Berlin.

—— (1986), 'Fertility and the Tax-Benefit System: A Reconsideration of the Theory of Family Taxation', *Economic Journal*, 96.

—— (1988*a*), 'Some Macroeconomic Consequences of the New Home Economics', in R. Lee, W. D. Arthur, and G. Rodgers (eds.), *Economics of Changing Age Distributions in Developed Countries*, Oxford University Press, Oxford.

—— (1988*b*), 'Cause e rimedi economici del calo della natalità', *Economia Politica*, 5.

—— (1989), 'The Timing of Births: A Theory of Fertility, Family Expenditures and Labour Market Participation over Time', in A. Wenig, and K. F. Zimmermann (eds.), *Demographic Change and Economic Development*, Springer-Verlag, Berlin.

—— (1990*a*), 'Home-Production and the Allocation of Time', in D. Sapsford and Z. Tzannatos (eds.), *Current Issues in Labour Economics*, Macmillan, London.

—— (1990*b*), 'Teoria economica della popolazione e transferimenti intergenerazionali: perche i sistemi persionistici a ripartizione sono intrinsecamente instabili', in F. R. Pizzuti and G. M. Rey (eds.), *Il Sistema Pensionistico*, Il Mulino, Bologna.

—— and Ermisch, J. (1989), 'A Microeconomic Analysis of the Timing of Births', *European Economic Review*, 31.

Coase, R. H. (1980), 'The Problem of Social Cost', *Journal of Law and Economics*, 3.

Colombino, U., and De Stavola, B. (1985), 'A Model of Female Labor Supply in Italy Using Cohort Data', *Journal of Labor Economics*, 3.

Deaton, A. S., and Muellbauer, J. (1986), 'On Measuring Child Costs: With Applications to Poor Countries', *Journal of Political Economy*, 94.

De Santis, G., and Righi, A. (1990), 'Measures of Child Cost in Italy', paper presented to the European Association for Population Studies Conference on *Familles et niveaux de vie: Observation et analyse*, Barcelona.

Diamond, P. A. (1977), 'A Framework for Social Security Analysis', *Journal of Public Economics*, 8.

DOLTON, P. J. (1982), 'The "Marriage Game": An Assignment Problem with Indivisibilities', *Theory and Decision*, 14.

ERMISCH, J. (1979), 'The Relevance of the Easterlin Hypothesis and the "New Home Economics" to Fertility Movements in Great Britain', *Population Studies*, 33.

―― (1981a), 'Economic Opportunities, Marriage Squeezes and the Propensity to Marry; An Economic Analysis of Period Marriage Rates in England and Wales', *Population Studies*, 36.

―― (1981b), 'An Economic Analysis of Household Formation, Theory and Evidence from the General Household Survey', *Scottish Journal of Political Economy*, 28.

―― (1987a), 'Impacts of Policy Actions on the Family', *Journal of Public Policy*, 6.

―― (1987b), 'Econometric Analysis of Birth Dynamics', Discussion Paper, National Institute of Economic and Social Research, London.

―― (1987c), 'The Economics of the Family: Application to Divorce and Remarriage', Discussion Paper, Centre for Economic Policy Research, London.

ESPENSHADE, T. J. (1984), *Investing in Children: New Estimates of Parental Expenditures*, The Urban Institute Press, Washington, DC.

FREIDEN, A. (1974), 'The U.S. Marriage Market', *Journal of Political Economy*, 81.

GALE, D., and SHAPLEY, L. (1962), 'College Admissions and the Stability of Marriage', *American Mathematical Monthly*, 69.

GROSSBARD-SHECHTMAN, A. (1984), 'A Theory of Allocation of Time in Markets for Labour and Marriage', *Economic Journal*, 94.

GUSTAFSSON, S. (1985), 'Institutional Environment and the Economics of Female Labor Force Participation and Fertility: A Comparison between Sweden and West Germany', Discussion Paper IIM/LMP 85-9, Wissenschaftszentrum, Berlin.

HALL, R. E., and LAZEAR, E. P. (1984), 'The Excess Sensitivity of Layoffs and Quits to Demand', *Journal of Labor Economics*, 2.

HAPPEL, S. K., HILL, J. K., and LOW, S. A. (1984), 'An Economic Analysis of the Timing of Childbirth'. *Population Studies*, 38.

HARBURY, C. D., and HITCHINS, D. M. W. N. (1979), *Inheritance and Wealth Inequality in Britain*, Allen and Unwin, London.

HASHIMOTO, M. H., and YU, B. T. (1980), 'Specific Capital,

Employment Contracts and Wage Rigidity', *Bell Journal of Economics*, 11.

HICKMAN, B. G. (1974), 'What Became of the Building Cycle', in P. David and M. Reder (eds.), *Nations and Households in Economic Growth: Essays in Honor of Moses Abramovitz*, Academic Press, New York.

HÖPFLINGER, F. (1984), 'Cohort Fertility in Western Europe: Comparing Trends in Recent Birth Cohorts', *Genus*, 40.

HOTZ, V. J., and MILLER, R. A. (1986), 'The Economics of Family Planning', Discussion Paper, Carnegie-Mellon University, Pittsburgh.

JOSHI, H. (1990), 'The Cash Opportunity-Cost of Childbearing: An Approach to Estimation Using British Data', *Population Studies*, 44.

KEELEY, M. C. (1977), 'The Economics of Family Formation', *Economic Enquiry*, 14.

—— (1979), 'An Analysis of the Age Pattern of First Marriage', *International Economic Review*, 20.

LANCASTER, K. (1966), 'A New Approach to Consumer Theory', *Journal of Political Economy*, 74.

LEE, R. D. (1980), 'Aiming at a Moving Target: Period Fertility and Changing Reproductive Goals', *Population Studies*, 34.

LEMENNICIER, B. (1988), *Le Marché du mariage et de la famille*, Presses Universitaires de France, Paris.

LUCE, R. and RAIFFA, H. (1957), *Games and Decisions*, Wiley, New York.

MANSER, M., and BROWN, M. (1980), 'Marriage and Household Decision-Making: A Bargaining Analysis', *International Economic Review*, 21.

MEADE, J. E. (1952), 'External Economies and Diseconomies in a Competitive Situation', *Economic Journal*, 62.

MINCER, J. (1962), 'Labor Force Participation of Married Women', in National Bureau of Economic Research, *Aspects of Labor Economics*, Princeton University Press, Princeton.

—— (1985), 'Intercountry Comparisons of Labor Force Trends and of Related Developments: An Overview', *Journal of Labor Economics*, 3 (supplement).

MIRER, T. (1980), 'The Dissaving Behaviour of the Retired Aged', *Southern Economic Journal*, 46.

MIRRLEES, J. A. (1971), 'An Exploration in the Theory of Optimum Income Taxation', *Review of Economic Studies*, 38.

—— (1972), 'Population Policy and the Taxation of Family Size', *Journal of Public Economics*, 1.

MOFFITT, R. (1984*a*), 'Optimal Life-Cycle Profiles of Fertility and Labor Supply', *Research in Population Economics*, 5.

—— (1984*b*), 'Profiles of Fertility, Labor Supply and Wages of Married Women: A Complete Life-Cycle Model' *Review of Economic Studies*, 51.

MONNIER, A. (1989), 'Le Conjoncture démographique', *Population*, 44.

MORTENSEN, D. T. (1978), 'Specific Capital and Labor Turnover', *Bell Journal of Economics*, 9.

MUÑOZ-PEREZ, F. (1986), 'Changements récents de la fécondité en Europe Occidentale et nouveaux traits de la formation des familles', *Population*, 41.

MUTH, F. (1966), 'Household Production and Consumer Demand Function', *Econometrica*, 34.

NERLOVE, M., RAZIŇ, A., and SADKA, E. (1987), *Household and Economy: Welfare Economics of Endogenous Fertility*, Academic Press, New York.

NEWMAN, J. (1983), 'A Stochastic Dynamic Model of Fertility', Discussion Paper, Tulane University, New Orleans.

PITCHFORD, J. (1974), *Population in Economic Growth*, North-Holland, Amsterdam.

—— (1985), 'External Effects of Population Growth', *Oxford Economic Papers*, 37.

POLLAK, R. A. (1985), 'A Transactions Cost Approach to Families and Households', *Journal of Economic Literature*, 23.

RAZIN, A. (1980), 'Number, Spacing and Quality of Children', *Research in Population Economics*, 2.

ROSENZWEIG, M. R., and SCHULTZ, T. P. (1985), 'The Demand for and Supply of Births: Fertility and its Life-Cycle Consequences', *American Economic Review*, 75.

SCHULTZ, T. P. (1976), 'An Economic Interpretation of the Decline in Fertility in a Rapidly Developing Country', in R. Easterlin (ed.), *Population and Economic Change in Developing Countries*, University of Chicago Press, Chicago.

SCHULTZ, T. W. (1974), 'Fertility and Economic Values', in T. W.

Schultz (ed.), *Economics of the Family*, University of Chicago Press, Chicago.

STIGLER, G. J., and BECKER, G. S. (1977), 'De gustibus non est disputandum', *American Economic Review*, 67.

TURCHI, B. A. (1975), *The Demand for Children: The Economics of Fertility in the United States*, Ballinger, Cambridge, Mass.

—— (1983), *Estimating the Cost of Children in the United States*, Final Report to the National Institutes of Child Health and Human Development, Carolina Population Centre, University of North Carolina at Chapel Hill.

WALKER, K. E., and WOODS, M. E. (1976), *Time Use: A Measure of Household Production of Family Goods and Services*, The American Home Economics Association, Washington, DC.

WEITZMAN, L. J. (1981), *The Marriage Contract: Spouses, Lovers and the Law*, Free Press, New York.

WILLIS, R. J. (1973), 'A New Approach to the Economic Theory of Fertility Behaviour', *Journal of Political Economy*, 81.

WINEGARDEN, C. R. (1984), 'Women's Fertility, Market Work and Marital Status: A Test of the New Household Economics with International Data', *Economica*, 51.

Index